Available Light

Philip Booth and the Gift of Place

JEANNE BRAHAM

BAUHAN PUBLISHING 2016
PETERBOROUGH * NEW HAMPSHIRE

ISBN: 978-0-87233-206-5

Library of Congress Cataloging-in-Publication Data
Names: Braham, Jeanne, 1940- author.
Title: Available light : Philip Booth and the gift of place / Jeanne Braham.
Description: Peterborough, New Hampshire : Bauhan Publishing, 2016. | Includes bibliographical references.
Identifiers: LCCN 2015042130 | ISBN 9780872332065 (softcover/gatefold : alk. paper)
Subjects: LCSH: Booth, Philip, 1925-2007. | Poets, American—20th century—Biography. | New England—Poetry.
Classification: LCC PS3552.O647 Z56 2015 | DDC 811/.54—dc23
LC record available at http://lccn.loc.gov/2015042130

Book design by Kirsty Anderson and Sarah Bauhan.
Cover design by Henry James.
Cover photo of "The Poet," 1987, Castine, Maine by Peter Ralston.
Photo of the author by Robert Floyd.
Printed at Kase Printing, Hudson, New Hampshire.

Manufactured in the United States of America.

For Margaret

Contents

Hatch Cove
Wadsworth Cove
Blockhouse Pt
Ft George
Hosp
SPIRE
CASTINE
Castine Harbor
Cable Area
Dice Head
Aband. Lt. Ho.
TOWER
12M
Rock Shoal
Piles
Middle Ground
Hosmer Ledge
Bn "2"
hrd
BW"CH" BELL
Nautilus I
Nautilus Rock
C"IA"
rky
Ram I
Holbrook I
Cable Area
stk

Available Light

As one walks down Castine's Main Street to the harbor,
the "water seems to rise up to meet you."

Introduction

September 2013: Late summer is giving way to October leaves and slanted light. I'm fortunate to have spent the last several days as the guest of Carol Booth, daughter of poet Philip Booth, visiting and absorbing the haunts—both literal and metaphoric—of her father's home in Castine, Maine. Classic Federalist and Greek Revival houses line Main Street, including this stately white multiple-chimneyed home in a community by the sea where Booth's family members have lived for five generations. The dazzling harbor lies at the foot of the steep hill, which drops so precipitously that, in the words of one resident, "the water seems to rise up to meet you." Eaton's Boatyard, subject of a famous Booth poem, and Dennett's Wharf remain the hub of the busy harbor area, and a bell tolls at regular intervals from the historic Trinitarian Church tower. The 500-foot *State of Maine*, a training vessel operated by the nearby Maine Maritime Academy, dwarfs the pleasure boats moored in the harbor. This weekend the academy is enjoying homecoming, and visitors who are not attending the football game are taking photographs of this impressive ship.

Located on a peninsula between the Penobscot River and the Bagaduce River, both of which empty into Penobscot Bay, Castine was a vigorously contested strategic settlement site for many years. The town is filled with signs describing the locations of massacres or vanished forts. Fort Pentagoet is the prime example: a French trading post in 1613, it changed hands nine times among the English, French, and Dutch explorers, traders, and military during the ensuing 130 years. As I am coming to learn, it is within this storied setting that Philip Booth's poems came alive in layered and nuanced ways.

I first encountered Philip Booth's poetry when I read, in a popular

95 Main Street, where Philip Booth's family has lived for five generations.

college poetry anthology of my era, "How to See Deer." The poem, now among his best known and originally published in the collection *Available Light*, works by reduction, stripping away the usual expectations one might have when stalking deer (presumably either to kill or to photograph). Quietly, carefully, the poet discards these expectations:

How to See Deer

Forget roadside crossings.
Go nowhere with guns.
Go elsewhere your own way,

lonely and wanting. Or
stay and be early:
next to deep woods

inhabit old orchards.
All clearings promise.
Sunrise is good,

and fog before sun.
Expect nothing always;
find your luck slowly.

Wait out the windfall.
Take your good time
to learn to read ferns;

make like a turtle:
downhill toward slow water.
Instructed by heron,

drink the pure silence.
Be compassed by wind.
If you quiver like aspen

trust your quick nature;
let your ear teach you
which way to listen.

You've come to assume
protective color; now
colors reform to

new shapes in your eye.
You've learned by now
to wait without waiting;

as if it were dusk
look into light falling:
in deep relief

things even out. Be
careless of nothing. See
what you see.

A hub of Castine's busy harbor area, Eaton's Boatyard is the subject of a well-known poem by Booth.

Even to my untutored undergraduate eye and ear, this poem seemed remarkable. It revealed what it was not (a poem about how to see a deer) by simultaneously revealing what it was: an exploration of how to "see / what you see." Accustomed to the directives (explicit and implicit) issued by many of the English professors of my generation to see / what *I* see, I found Booth's invitation to the reader both an open-ended gift and a daunting challenge.

The economy of line and image, the propulsion of the enjambed lines whose meanings spill into the next stanza and the next, the trust extended to the reader—all of this sent me in search of all the other Philip Booth poems I could find. Years later, when I found myself on the other side of the classroom desk, I shared Booth's poems with four decades of college students. Many of them were drawn to the urgency of his compressed poetic forms, the precision with which he uses language—especially verbs—and his enticing habit of alluding to more by saying less. To discuss Booth's poems was to participate in the making of their meaning(s), to be electrified by the possibilities.

He published ten volumes of meticulously crafted lyric poems in his lifetime, stretching from *Letter from a Distant Land*, in 1957, to *Lifelines*, in 1999. Like other major poets writing from New England who were

On the wharf at Eaton's Boatyard, looking out to sea.

his contemporaries—Richard Wilbur, Maxine Kumin, Stanley Kunitz, Donald Hall—the echoes of Robert Frost register in his structure and language. Booth knew Frost personally, studying with him first at Dartmouth, where Booth's father was a professor in the English Department and where Frost spent several months annually as a writer-in-residence. Gradually they developed a friendship, and when Booth went to Columbia to do graduate work with Mark Van Doren, Frost was the subject of his master's thesis. Frost's use of the vernacular New England speaking voice—its cadences, emphases, and pauses—turns up in Booth's use of the habits of mind and speech patterns of Down East Maine. And when Booth says of Frost's famous poem, "Desert Places," that "the poem is not only the poem of the words, but the poem of the empty spaces between them,"[1] he could well be describing any number of his own poems.

If Frost served as a poetic mentor and steadfast friend until his death in 1963, Castine provided the historic, geographic, and experiential canvas upon which Booth's poems are painted.

As Joan Didion contends, "a place belongs forever to whoever claims it the hardest, remembers it most obsessively, wrenches it from itself, shapes it, renders it, loves it so radically that he remakes it in his own image." Booth claimed Castine fervently. "What I write," he said, "is rooted in this house, this street, this town. I'm positive that I received at least as much education on Dennett's Wharf between the ages of six and 18, as I got from four years of college and a year of graduate school."[2] He seems to have intuited early that knowledge of Castine came from working in it in all seasons, suffering its hardships, loving its advantages, and valuing the friends and family who had invested love and labor in it before. By the time his second book, *The Islanders,* was published, his poems had come to depend, in immediate and sensory ways, on the geography of coastal Maine and the activities associated with living there: rowing boats, navigating through thick fog that obscured normal landmarks, recording the talk of wharf workers, splitting wood and methodically stacking it. Living intimately with the land and with the sea was a way of *paying attention*, the special province of a poet. And, as his subsequent poetic explorations demonstrated,

The view from Booth's second floor writing studio includes tree-lined Main Street as well as the yellow home of next-door neighbors Mary McCarthy and James West.

honoring and describing an exterior landscape triggered a way of finding an interior landscape.

While some Castine residents, like Booth's maternal ancestors, the Hookes, shared decades of Castine's history, others, like Peter Davis, a documentary filmmaker and writer, were attracted to the community both for its history and for its sizable arts community. Painters, sculptors, historians, theologians, and especially writers began gathering in the 1950s, '60s, and '70s, and anchored by the presence of Philip Booth; next-door neighbor Mary McCarthy and her husband, former diplomat James West; and writers Robert "Cal" Lowell, and his wife, Elizabeth "Lizzie" Hardwick, Castine gained a reputation as a first-rate artists' colony. Booth, at times, seemed bemused by the visitors who flocked to Castine, who were sometimes, as he puts it in a journal entry, "pressured by Cal Lowell or Mary McCarthy to visit."

He wrote, "[It can] sound like a guest-list out of *Gatsby*: Bill Meredith for a day or a week at a time, Bill and Dido Merwin most of one summer; Rollie McKenna with her Nikons, Andy and Pat Wanning, Elizabeth Bishop for the best of a week. . . ."[3] Despite the madcap feel of things at times, it seems clear from their journals and letters that the quartet of Booth, McCarthy, Lowell, and Hardwick embarked on a particularly productive period from the late '50s to the early '70s during which their friendships deepened, their individual writing projects flourished, and they enjoyed one another's company on sailing trips, picnics, and frequent dinner parties. Each writer's work was energized, in part, because of the support and stimulation offered by the others.

Henry Miller, who spent his childhood summers in Castine and who took sailing lessons from Booth, remembers him less as one of the literary luminaries and more as

> *. . . a part of the waterfront landscape, similar in many ways to the boatbuilders and dockworkers whom he so enjoyed. He was reserved, spoke when he had something to say.*
>
> *To me he was primarily observant: he watched what was happening around him, who was there, and what was said, but he saw it all in the minutest details: What tools were on the bench? What skills were required? What instincts were needed? What words were used? In my mind, he saw the words, as they were used; he didn't just hear them. They were visible, and he could touch them and claim the ones he needed for later use.*[4]

If Booth was "primarily observant," his interests in photography and in painting were logical extensions of the particulars that triggered his imagination. He loved photography, documenting daily events through his own snapshots, and he spoke of fine art photography as "writing with light." And as poet Wesley McNair observed:

> *Booth was drawn to painters, particularly Fitz Hugh Lane and John Marin, who repeatedly painted the Maine coast. They were*

> *seeing the same coast everybody else was seeing, but revealing it in an entirely new way.*
>
> *John Marin, celebrated in Booth's poem "Sea-Change," is a painter whose approach is, like Booth's, suggestive and poetic, who is also an inveterate framer, often adding to the picture—up to three additional frames applied by paint—just as Booth adds to the structure of the line and regular stanza a carefully structured language, frames within the frame.*[5]

Booth's own photograph albums—large well-worn books that the Booth family generously allowed me to see and later to scan for use in this portrait—and his habit of carefully documenting the images with names, dates, locations, and sometimes even snippets of conversation, suggest that he may have used these volumes as sourcebooks, as visual equivalents of the written journals he kept and called "commonplace books."

Although honors commensurate with his talent came steadily his way—including Guggenheim, Rockefeller, and National Endowment for the Arts fellowships, as well as the Theodore Roethke Prize and election to the Academy of American Poets—and although many ranked him among the major American poets writing in the latter half of the twentieth century, Booth's life and body of work have yet to receive the comprehensive critical attention that some of his peers have enjoyed. Some attribute this to his decision not to participate in public readings at a time when readings became the primary way poets developed a wide readership for their work. In order to bolster a career in poetry, a poet needed to become a public face; either readings did not appeal to Booth, or he was temperamentally ill-suited to do them with ease. On the other hand, part of what endeared Booth to poet Richard Wilbur, a fellow teacher at Wellesley, was precisely his unwillingness to trim his sail to fit the prevailing winds of the day. "He was always his own man, and I admired that," said Wilbur. Maxine Kumin echoed Wilbur's words: "Booth's work has a wonderfully consistent tone; he has pursued his destiny as a poet in an understated and unswerving way. His deeply rooted sense of place is reflected in poem after poem—not so much about the landscape of coastal Maine, but about its outreach, its human dimension.” As Booth himself observed, “Being a poet is not a career, it’s a life. Writing poems is not a career but a lifetime of looking into, and listening to, how words see.”[6] Surely it is time to document that life and to explore some of the incandescent poems that emerged from it.

Thoreau, whom Booth called “my distant kin,” insisted that the geography of place and the geography of the spirit are one terrain. I was reminded of that when Carol Booth and I visited the town cemetery to see her father’s grave. It is set into a gently sloped hillside, backed by trees, and facing the harbor. The headstone is modest and contains these words, written by Booth, succinct and resonant:

PHILIP BOOTH

WHO LOVED CASTINE

IN ALL HIS DAYS

OCTOBER 8, 1925–JULY 2, 2007

In order to explore the arc of Booth’s life and work, I knew Castine was the place to begin and to end.

First Lesson

Philip Edmund Booth was a quintessential New Englander, growing up in Hanover, New Hampshire, a scenic college town bordering the Connecticut River, home to Dartmouth College, and also in Castine, Maine, a historic seaside village located on the shores of Penobscot Bay. His father, Edmund Booth, a professor of literature and writing at Dartmouth College (also Philip Booth's alma mater), lived with his wife, Jean, son Philip, and daughter, Lee, close to the college campus. They habitually summered in Castine in the big white clapboard house on Main Street that belonged to Jean's family. (Philip's maternal great-great-grandfather had been appointed by Thomas Jefferson to serve as customs collector in Castine, and subsequent members of Jean's family—the Hookes—lived in the community thereafter.) In an interview in Castine

Booth with his maternal grandparents in the formal garden behind the Castine house.

with Philip Conkling, Booth remembered growing up in the ancestral home during boyhood summers.

> *I had an imposing Victorian grandmother who was a rather fearsome presence in this house, and yet she was a very engaging and intelligent woman. She'd gone to school in Portland before marrying my grandfather—a marriage that was somehow arranged; I'm not sure just how. He was ill in this house a long time. I think he wished to be a carpenter, and my grandmother didn't feel it fit her standing. So I think he went into depressions and stayed upstairs in the house mostly—although I remember him as the man I called Oman, as in "Oh man, oh man, pay attention to me!" when I was a little boy.*
>
> *I cannot claim to be a native. I came here* in utero *on the Boston boat, as a matter of fact, like a thousand other people. I'm reminded every day by appropriate friends here that I am not native. And I don't pretend to be. But one of the great things about growing up here was having a man come out of the post office one day, 20 years ago, and saying, "Aren't you Jean Hookes'*

"Oman, as in 'Oh man, oh man, pay attention to me'."

boy?" "Yup, yup." He said, "Your name Philip Hooke?" I said, "No, Philip Booth, but that's the right Hooke." He said, "He was your grandfather?" I said, "No, he was my great-grandfather." "Well, " he says, "I want to tell you, he was the person that came down these steps right here at the post office and told me they'd sunk the Maine."

That's lovely. I like that a lot. That does resonate, the way sailing up the bay does and knowing that, although not in my direct line, my great-great uncles and people like that saw pretty much this coast as it still is (or was until the last 15 or 20 years ago.)[1]

If the fact that he was a part of five generations of his family rooted in Castine resonated in his consciousness, the fact that he was born in

The aspiring author, about age 4.

Hanover with close ties to Dartmouth College brought him into Robert Frost's orbit. During his high school years, Booth attended Vermont Academy and was attracted to literature, to tennis, and to skiing—"in about equal measure." It was largely through his father's love of poetry and friendship with Robert Frost that Booth became seriously interested in poetry.

> *In the fall of 1942 I was away at school in Vermont Academy, beginning my senior year. Because the war was on, we took the first week of school to help harvest the apple crop in southern Vermont.*

That was hard work of a kind I'd never done before. My father (Bless him!) sent me a typed copy of a Frost poem called "After Apple-Picking." I'd been mildly interested in poetry before, but not very much; about one third as much as most high school students who become poets. But here was a poet who didn't talk like Shelley or Byron or anybody. Here was Frost saying: "My instep arch not only keeps the ache; it keeps the pressure of the ladder round." And it suddenly occurred to me that poets could tell the truth! I was hooked on that realization. . . .

When I went off to the Air Corps a few years later, my father thought to send me a book of Frost's poems, and he asked Frost to sign it. Mr. Frost said, "Who's it for?" And when my father told him, he said, "Is he the one I talked to in the library last year?" My father said, "Yes." Mr. Frost said, "I'll go buy him a book myself." And he went stumping across the street to the Dartmouth Bookstore and bought it and sent it to me.

After the war I went back and saw him. Mr. Frost asked, "What did you do during the war? Did you kill anybody?" I said, "No, about the only thing I did was meet the girl in Georgia who I'm going to marry next summer." "You're going to marry her, huh?," he said. "Yup." He said, "When she gets accustomed to it, have her ask me to tea." He was very kind to us during those early years.[2]

While Booth's own experiments in poetic form and narrative voice would depart from the Frost model, his work, like that of most of the poets of his generation (especially those writing in and about New England), would always bear the imprint of Frost's legacy: a New England landscape that is not merely "a setting" but an emotional and psychological context contributing to the poem's meaning; a clear commitment to form, without which poetry would be, in Frost's words, "like playing tennis without a net"; and the belief that poetry is not didactic, but rather a vehicle for providing an experience that then develops out of its own inevitabilities—riding, as Frost would put it, like "a piece of ice on a hot stove . . . on its own melting."

Booth also felt affinities to Frost's temperament, often applying

"Puritan to the bone" to his own habits of mind and heart. By using that phrase, he was not claiming the dour, stern rigidity associated with the Puritan stereotype. And he certainly was not consciously claiming the fear-haunted admonitions of Jonathan Edwards's "Sinners in the Hands of an Angry God," those attitudes that H. L. Mencken mocked when he defined the essence of Puritanism as "the haunting fear that someone, somewhere, may be happy." Frost, in claiming a Puritan heritage, was describing a sensibility sometimes named "Yankee": a kind of hovering skepticism, a quality of ironic detachment, a wry, laconic response to the good and bad of one's daily life, a healthy respect for individual eccentricity, the daily desire to do something useful. Some of these same traits Booth used as definers of his own temperament. As he said in the poem "Adding It Up":

> I'm Puritan to the bone, down to
> the marrow and then some:
> if I'm not sorry I worry,
> if I can't worry I count.

Like a number of his Dartmouth classmates, Booth enlisted in the military—in his case, in the Air Corps—in the early 1940s, where he met Margaret Tillman, the "girl in Georgia" he intended to marry. Upon his discharge, he returned to Dartmouth to complete his BA, marrying Margaret after she, too, had completed her college degree. He remembers those years as exploratory, a time when "I was trying on different selves"; he trained in a woodworking shop, he tutored, he taught skiing and went on the road as a ski boot salesman, and, after receiving an MA at Columbia, he taught briefly at Bowdoin College and then served as assistant director of admissions at Dartmouth. Margaret remembers:

> *We didn't marry very quickly, but really were rather sensible in getting to know one another and completing college. I was a student at Wesleyan Conservatory of Music in Macon, Georgia, studying piano, when I met Philip. Macon, situated in close proximity to a number of military training bases, was a hub for servicemen in those years: Navy, Army, Air Force were all there. On some occasions students from the conservatory would offer musical*

Robert Frost and the young Booth at Dartmouth College Library, 1946.

> *programs, usually in private homes, to entertain servicemen who were in town. On this particular occasion the Air Force Glee Club was also performing, and Philip had a good friend who was a member of that group. That's how we met. Philip and I were very fortunate to know a family who lived in Macon and who were old friends of the Booth family—and they invited us to meet often in their home, enjoy their children (a daughter and son, fourteen and eight), and get to know one another. But after this romantic interlude, Philip had to finish his stint in the Air Corps, then go back to finish at Dartmouth. I needed to graduate from Wesleyan, after which I went back home for a brief time. My mother and I were invited to Hanover thereafter, where we met the Booth family and enjoyed seeing the New England landscape. Philip and I were engaged after that visit.*
>
> *Philip's first teaching job was at Bowdoin and it was brief. The English Department seemed especially embattled the year he was there and he left quickly, deciding to take his master's degree at Columbia. I found New York City very glamorous and exciting, though I don't think Philip was crazy about it. And I found myself doing something I could never have imagined myself doing: I got a job at a very sophisticated department store on Fifth Avenue, modeling beautiful clothes—walking around, showing the customers the latest fashionable wear. When I look back on that year, I'm still a little stunned. But it was such fun.*[3]

As Margaret suspected, her husband had a somewhat different response to the year in New York. He admitted years later, "I am not a very good traveler. I like to know every aspect of my locality, wherever it is. When I lived in New York for a year, I would often take the subway from Times Square to Columbia University. It bothered me very much that even though I followed the green or red lights (whichever they were then) to get the subway from Times Square to the university, it seemed to me when I sat in the subway that it took off backwards, because I thought I was facing north. I was making a wrong turn in my head. And I was even so curious as to take a compass with me once to find out where I was making that wrong turn in my head. Of course there was too much

Margaret and Philip Booth, 1955.

metal underground and I could not find where true north was anyway. I tell this only as an indication of how surely I like to know where I am. Only when I in some sense feel that I know where I am, am I able to look down into as well as to look out toward."[4]

Margaret had her own adjustments to make, accommodating not only to life "in the North," but also to Down East life and the tightly knit community of Castine. When Booth took her to Castine for the first time, or so the story goes, he took her down to Eaton's Boatyard, the hub of the harbor area, owned and operated at that time by Mace Eaton. "Mace looked her over and promptly asked her, in his thick guttural Maineaccented voice, if she liked salt-cod. When she indicated she wasn't sure, he grabbed a piece of salted fish that was hanging off of a nail on the back of the shed and offered it to her. She gamely ate a bite or two, proclaimed it good, and passed the test. Word spread pretty quickly throughout the town that Philip Booth had not only come home from the war, but that he had also brought home a pretty special girl from Georgia."[5]

It was not until Booth came to a full-time academic position at Wellesley College in 1954, setting up residence in nearby rural Lincoln, that he felt something like "true north": what he called "the surge," the excitement of other gifted poets who were teaching and writing in the Boston area. At the center of this exciting circle of young and promising poets was John Holmes, a teacher and poetry-workshop leader at Tufts University. Although Holmes achieved some success as a poet himself, his greatest gift was as a behind-the-scenes facilitator. He was tireless

The 1955 University of New Hampshire Writing Conference Staff:
Booth is seated, lower left, and John Holmes, upper right.

in connecting and fostering the careers of younger, emerging poets. He taught evening poetry workshops at the Boston Center for Adult Education, as well as at Tufts and the University of New Hampshire at Durham; in the summers he taught at Chautauqua Institution in New York State—and through his wide-ranging contacts he made a number of these teaching opportunities available to younger poets.

He also hosted a poetry circle in his own home in Medford; the group, which included, at various times, Richard Wilbur, John Ciardi, May Sarton, George Starbuck, Donald Hall, Anne Sexton, and Maxine Kumin, read and discussed each other's poems. He began a television program on WGBH-TV, assisted by Philip Booth and Donald Hall. As Booth remembers, "The three of us would trade poems and talk about them on TV. In fact we ran three dummy programs and they were a lot of fun, and then we did a fourth and we began getting fan mail from Winthrop and Hartford and everywhere else and we were terrified. Television was so new and we went off the air very soon."[6]

Donald Hall remembers that brief foray into Boston Public Television as "just the three of us [Holmes, Booth, Hall] sitting around a table talking, I think rather boringly, about poetry. I have much more vivid memories of Phil, while he was teaching at Wellesley and I was living in Lexington, when he came to my house and we sat together in my basement workroom, and talked talked talked."[7]

Robert Frost was by far the most visible poet in the Boston area at that time. As Peter Davison describes it, Frost "characteristically spent several months each year, spring and fall, at his house at 35 Brewster Street in Cambridge. . . . When Frost was in Cambridge—say, late March until June, and October until Christmas—he took his place at the center of Boston literary life. . . . Every October he gave a poetry reading at Tufts University for his friend John Holmes; he usually gave a reading at Harvard or Boston University or Boston College as well as Tufts, in fact as many colleges as his stamina and their budgets would allow."[8] With emerging poets of the caliber of Hall, Kunitz, Adrienne Rich, Kumin, Sexton, Sylvia Plath, and Ted Hughes; the growing reputation of poets like W. S. Merwin, Lowell, and Wilbur; and the support and sponsorship of an influential figure like Holmes and a towering figure like Frost, it's scant

John Holmes's photo of Ted Hughes and Sylvia Plath,
taken at the Booth home in Lincoln, 1957.

Dr. Marion Booth, Booth's aunt, who was Plath's
psychiatrist at Smith College, 1954.

wonder that Booth described this heady time in the late '50s as "a surge."

Although Philip Booth spoke of John Holmes with clear gratitude and credited the readings Holmes arranged as stimulants to his poetic experimentation, he developed his own craft almost exclusively on his own. "I traded poems with Holmes, casually," he said. "But I didn't trade much with other poets. Fundamentally, I've always been more of a loner than my colleagues. I really wasn't a part of his reading circle, though he did sign me on to coach the B team at the Boston Center for Adult Education. I did have a book out by then, so perhaps I was considered one step ahead. I do remember meeting Sylvia [Plath] after a Hughes reading. My aunt was her doctor at Smith, Dr. Marion Booth, the first woman psychiatrist ever appointed to be a college physician anywhere. When Sylvia and Ted moved to Boston we certainly went to their home and they came to ours several times. Late in the spring of 1959 we went out with them to Annisquam, a long day, one of those cold spring picnics."[9]

As he told Philip Conkling:

> *We were living in Lincoln and I was teaching at Wellesley when I wrote most of the poems in my first book,* Letter from a Distant Land. *If it seems that many of those poems were written about or during the hours of darkness, it is because when our girls were young I certainly had to wait for night before I could write very much. I simply cannot imagine now how I wrote that book in a small house when we had three small children and I was teaching at Wellesley. The answer is Margaret, I'm sure. I wrote mostly at night for many years, or in early morning dark.*[10]

But beyond the actual time of composition, another kind of darkness suffused many of Booth's poems, one he was aware of from the beginning. "There's a realm of darkness in all of us. Most of us know some of it. Which, being a part of our lives, seems to me as worth exploring as any other part. Each in his/her own darkness. Loneliness. Isolations. The ways through."[11]

A connection with Robert Frost, years earlier, helped Booth define personal darkness, an incident when "Mr. Frost gave me a glimpse of his night side."

> *He was close to seventy-five. I had just started to think about words: there were better than fifty years between us. . . . Mr. Frost and I had talked alone that night in the Hanover Inn until eleven, but when I got up to leave he waved his hand negatively across his chest: "No," he said, "I'll walk you home." I remember the heaved town sidewalks; what we talked about I don't remember at all. I only know that when we got to my corner, more than half a mile from the Inn, I again said good-night.*
>
> *Mr. Frost shook his head. "I walked you home, now comes your turn. You have to walk me home."*
>
> *It was night, late, dark; the issue was, at heart, though I barely then realized it, how to part and get home through more night, toward whatever sleep would come later.*
>
> *Back and forth, forth and back. We walked East Wheelock Street four times at least, maybe six. Mr. Frost stopped, stood talking, and decided: "Enough for one night." He reached out to shake hands. "You go your way, I'll go mine."*
>
> *That was all. I guessed that I'd been initiated. But into what, beyond Mr. Frost's trust, I was far from sure. There were a good number of those nights over the next twelve years: Maine, Bread Loaf, Cambridge. But only when I myself lay sleepless, shaken, and empty in the attic room of another inn, the night before Mr. Frost's funeral, did I realize how often he had walked me (and many others) forth and back to being halfway home.*[12]

It was during his years at Wellesley that Booth embarked on an almost four-year period of classical Freudian psychoanalysis, driving five days a week from his classes in Wellesley to Boston for his sessions. For those familiar with Booth's boyhood memories, his decision to enter analysis came as no surprise. "The stories of Philip's boyhood summers in Castine were about much more than sailing and swimming and exploring. There was a shadow in that house," according to Patrick Walker, Booth's former son-in-law. "Philip's grandmother was a strict and formidable Victorian lady, given to hosting big teas in the formal gardens of the backyard. Her husband, suffering from depression or maybe agoraphobia, became a kind of invalid, remaining upstairs, sitting in the front bedroom in a rocker facing the window and occasionally waving to passersby. These were Jean's parents; Jean herself was very beautiful, shy, an only child, and suffered her own episodes of fragile health and withdrawal. This couldn't have been lost on Philip."[13] Characterizing the Booth years immediately preceding Wellesley, Peter Davison wrote flatly that Philip's mother, after suffering several breakdowns, "had become seriously ill and died in a mental hospital; in the summer of 1957 he [Philip] began his long struggle to mourn her death."[14]

The Castine landscape, in effect his "mother's land," provided the raw materials for two poems that explore his struggle to grieve her loss: "Storm in a Formal Garden" and "Chart 1203," both of which appear in *Letter from a Distant Land.*

"Storm in a Formal Garden" uses as its central metaphors the garden outside the Castine house—planted by Booth's grandmother and tended faithfully by his mother, geometric in design, with flowers chosen for their color and regular blooming patterns—and a thunderstorm that leaves the dreamscape cloaked in darkness, yet illumined by sudden flashes of light.

Storm in a Formal Garden

Where my struck mother stays,
she wakes to thunderstorms
of doubt. Squalls blacken
her bright-surfaced dreams,
and she stands coldly shaken,
lost in the dripping trees.

The weather shuts and opens:
horizon lightning traps
her in a quick exposure
of old fears; she trips
and rises twice unsure.
No one knows how it happens.

Where my dark mother waits
for sun, the wet slate sky
builds prison thunderheads,
and she, mired in anxiety,
must bear the drumroll nights
struck mute by what she dreads.

Her numb-mouthed silences
are desperate prayer, or else
the panic count from flash
to thunderclap. Impulse
fires her woman flesh,
and fevers her thin balances.

Miles from where my mother
falls, in that rank formal
garden that I bend
to weed, the wrens chirp normal
pleasure on the wind,
wrens scale the turning weather.

Weeds like conscience clog
my rake. My mother craves
more love than any son
can give. And I, with leaves
jammed on a sharpened tine,
sweat where my two hearts tug.

Dreams from her, I wake
beyond my mother's hope
and will. Beyond the son
I was, and the thunder's shape,
I clear the overgrown
last path my heart must rake.

"Chart 1203: Penobscot Bay and Approaches," is a poem that "any sailor navigating into Castine would recognize as full of truths," according to photographer Peter Ralston, himself an excellent waterman along the coast of Maine. How to navigate in treacherous water offered Booth his central metaphor. The longer, looser, lifting lines contrast sharply with the imprisoned lines Booth uses in "Storm in a Formal Garden," and suggest the lift and roll of the waves—as well as their peril.

Chart 1203

Penobscot Bay and Approaches

Whoever works a storm to windward, sails
in rain, or navigates in island fog,
must reckon from the slow swung lead, from squalls

on cheek; must bear by compass, chart, and log.
Parallels are ruled from compass rose
to known red nun: but still the landfall leg

risks set of tide, lost buoys, and breakers' noise
on shore where no shore was. Whoever plots
his homing on these Eastward islands knows

how Sou'west smoke obscures the sunny charts,
how gulls cry on a numberless black spar.
Where North is West of North, not true, he pilots

best who feels the coast for standpipe, spire,
tower, or stack, who owns local knowledge of shoal
or ledge, whose salt nose smells the spruce shore.

Where echoes drift, where the blind groundswell
clangs an iron bell, his fish-hook hand
keeps steady on the helm. He weathers rainsquall,

linestorm, fear, who bears away from the sound
of sirens wooing him to the cape's safe lee.
He knows the ghostship bow, the sudden headland

immanent in fog; but where rocks wander, he
steers down the channel that his courage
dredges. He knows the chart is not the sea.

Years later, when speaking about his mother's illness and death, Booth revealed, "Her death there [in a mental hospital] was my own fall out of Eden. When my mother broke and died, I was soon lost in my lostness. Within several years after her death it caught up with me very hard, so that I myself got pretty shaky, and by great good fortune went into psychoanalysis as a control."[15]

Psychoanalysis was, in the 1950s and '60s, an exploratory path sought by a number of writers and artists. Sometimes the agony of life experience and the urgency of inner turmoil drove the repeated hospitalizations and long-term treatments of poets such as Lowell, Sexton, Plath, and John Berryman. But just as frequently, psychoanalysis appealed to writers and artists who were struggling to excavate past experiences and sharpen their expressions of them—who were trying, as Booth liked to say, "not to tell lies." As Maxine Kumin, who was undergoing analysis at about the same time as Booth, suggests, "Analysis was a way of freeing me to write the poems I wanted and needed to write: it dared me to become a poet."

Booth's subsequent books dealt less directly with his mother's turmoil and his own sense of loss. Yet years after his analysis, he continued to log his dreams—and not primarily as fodder for poems. "I just want to keep in touch with my inner self, so that when I'm in hard weather, I'll know where it's coming from," he said.[16] Centering summer life in Castine—its familiar history, its topography, its people—offered both comfort and stimulation, the ideal conditions in which his art could grow. "Keeping in touch with my inner self" lies at the heart of most Booth poems, and a keen sense of place was one antidote to "lostness." When asked about Castine's enduring place in his poems, Booth said, "I think it was a matter of mooring myself in a known harbor, in order to sail out from it."[17]

Living in Lincoln during the winter months, with its proximity to Concord and Walden Pond, prompted Booth to reread *Walden*, to chuckle over the immaturity of his marginal notes in his high school Modern Library copy of the book, and to hike with his dog, Peter, around the pond. He was struck afresh by Thoreau's line: "Not till we are lost . . . do we begin to find ourselves, and realize where we are and the infinite extent of our relations." He thought about Thoreau's image of dropping a stone in the pond and watching the effect of rippling, concentric circles moving outward from the center, and of fellow poet Stanley Kunitz's conviction that "the universe is a continuous web. Touch it at any point and the whole web quivers."

Thoreau's appeal was multifaceted: Booth admired Thoreau's efforts to explore the microcosm in order to understand the macrocosm, to place his trust in tradesmen and makers of things rather than in institutions or governments, to endeavor to "drive life into a corner, and reduce it to its lowest terms, and if it proved mean, why then to get

Booth walking with his dog, Peter, around Walden Pond, 1955.

the whole and genuine meanness of it, and publish its meanness to the world; or if it were sublime, to know it by experience, and be able to give a true account of it. . . ."

Even Thoreau's eccentricities and love of solitude resonated with Booth, for in some of those qualities he found elements of himself: "I think I am something of an odd stick. I think I am fundamentally a loner, although I have better protective coloration in social contexts than Thoreau did. . . . In some sense I've always been certain of where my roots were. But only more recently have I become aware of Thoreau's sense of the 'infinite extent of our relations.'"[18] That everything exists in relation led Booth to ponder more complicated connections between the inner and outer territory expressed in his poems. The making of poems required more than a careful matching of life's particulars with a subject worthy of exploration; it demanded finding the connective tissue that releases the subject. His painstaking pursuit of that connective tissue

Carol and Margot on their new skis, Christmas, 1956.

Booth with Carol and Margot.

informed later work, especially the poems in *Relations, Selves,* and *Pairs.*

Parenthood was also a way of experiencing "the infinite extent of our relations." With the birth of daughters Margot, Carol, and Robin during the seven years in Lincoln, Booth found himself functioning not only as a mentor/parent in the college classroom, but also as the flesh-and-blood father to three lively, inquisitive, energetic little girls.

As Carol remembered: "There was not too much direct parenting. That came from my mother. But Dad liked to teach us things—how to ski, how to sail. He had a particular method, and that was to introduce us to the direct experience almost immediately. We learned to sail when Dad put the tiller in our hands. We learned to ski almost as soon as we could stand and keep our balance. I remember going down little hills in our backyard in Lincoln almost as soon as I could walk. And his lessons came also from the power of his own example. Since he was a tall, fit person, at home in his body, he loved to do sports where your body becomes part of executing the sport well: hiking out over the edge of a boat, executing the perfect downhill run by shifting your weight at just the right moment."[19]

One of Booth's most oft-quoted poems, "First Lesson," has as its nominal subject teaching a child how to float, how to feel comfortable in the water. But in an interview with Rachel Berghash, Booth suggested that:

> *I meant it to be far more metaphorical than literal. The instruction resonates with all of the hopes that one might have for a young daughter—including some fictions as well. I myself was not teaching my daughter to swim. I was watching a young woman, perhaps 18 or 20 years old, teach her to swim in a village swimming program in a little town in Vermont one summer. I noticed the instructress's hand cupping my daughter's head. And I realized how often I had done that, whether holding her as a baby or putting her up on my shoulder. Obviously such head holding may be a part of making love and I realized how she was moving toward that age. If there is instruction in art, it is best when implicit, perhaps even subliminal, I would say."*[20]

First Lesson

Lie back, daughter, let your head
be tipped back in the cup of my hand.
Gently, and I will hold you. Spread
your arms wide, lie out on the stream
and look high at the gulls. A dead-
man's-float is face down. You will dive
and swim soon enough where this tidewater
ebbs to the sea. Daughter, believe
me, when you tire on the long thrash
to your island, lie up, and survive.
As you float now, where I held you
and let go, remember when fear
cramps your heart what I told you:
lie gently and wide to the light-year
stars, lie back, and the sea will hold you.

Norwich swimming pool lesson, July 1956, an early study for what becomes the poem "First Lesson."

Teaching claimed a great deal of Booth's time during the Wellesley years. Liberal arts institutions have traditionally weighed classroom performance as heavily as independent research and writing—so much was expected of a young instructor: heavy class loads, significant advising time, independent study projects, and, for those instructors teaching writing and literature courses, grading an avalanche of papers each and every semester. In Booth's letters to friends and fellow writers, he commented with some frequency on the "demands of this semester" or the "weight of papers accumulating in my office." He was as careful and selective in preparing for a class as he was when preparing to write a poem; he turned back papers promptly, with both marginal comments and several paragraphs of summary commentary, rendered in his laser-cut handwriting.

Peter Davis, Johanna "Josie" Mankiewicz Davis, and their young sons.

Peter Davis, while a young undergraduate at Harvard, went to Wellesley to visit a childhood friend, Johanna "Josie" Mankiewicz, a student there who enrolled in several classes taught by Philip Booth. Josie was a colorful figure, talented and wildly funny, a woman who, in Peter's phrase, "could capture the room with her wit." She'd grown up in the Hollywood hills, the daughter of writer Herman Mankiewicz, who collaborated with Orson Welles on *Citizen Kane*. Peter's parents, also screenwriters, moved to Beverly Hills when Peter was about ten. He and Josie were, as he puts it, "fellow Hollywood brats." What he discovered when he went to visit Josie at Wellesley was not only what a compelling teacher Philip Booth was, though still quite young, but how utterly smitten Josie was with him.

Josie was taking a course in literature and poetry's traditions and it was taught by Philip Booth. She avowed that Booth was the most wonderful teacher she had ever heard and urged me to attend class with her. The first thing that I noticed was the way he looked. He was, at that time, the most handsome man I ever saw, outside of Gregory Peck. In fact, he reminded me of Gregory Peck, not necessarily in facial expressions, but in demeanor: the authority with which he spoke and carried himself, the deliberateness with which he chose words, his long, lean body, the way he'd gesture and punctuate his sentences by waving his pipe as if it were a prop.

He was talking that day about the play Oedipus Rex. Now we've all studied that play at one time or another and know the horror at its core: that Oedipus comes to realize that he has killed his father and is sleeping with his mother, and in his horror, blinds himself. Philip said something about that moment that I've never forgotten: "Oedipus lost his outlook, but gained insight." I thought that was wonderful. Though that moment was fifty-eight years ago, it still resonates for me.

Josie had a mad crush on him and would devise all sorts of excuses to go in and see him during his office hours. One day she had some pretext to go in, some comment on a paper, some oh-could-you-explain-Mr.-Booth-what-you-mean sort of thing. She sat rapt while he elucidated. And eventually, when she ran out of questions, she stood by the door. Perhaps it was time for a holiday break and she knew he'd be going home to his family and she to hers—and finally she blurted out, "Mr. Booth, Mr. Booth, there's something I have to tell you. I—I love you."

She said Philip never missed a beat, but smiled warmly and said smoothly, "Well, Johanna, that's very nice. And I love you too. And Margaret loves you, and Margot loves you, and Carol loves you too." I've always admired how he handled that—how deftly and gently in the face of all that vulnerability. But it must have been a little lost on Josie: her crush remained strong. She told me, "When I found out that Margaret was pregnant with Robin, I said out loud: 'Mr. Booth, you've been unfaithful to me.'"

Eventually Josie became Peter Davis's wife; they had two sons and settled in New York City. After Davis served an apprenticeship in TV documentaries, he wrote and produced for CBS *The Selling of the Pentagon*, which won an Emmy and a Peabody Award. But soon after he received the Peabody, tragedy struck: Josie was hit and killed by a taxi that had mounted a Greenwich Village sidewalk and veered directly into her path.

> *Josie and I never got to Castine together, but we knew Castine was a celestial place, both geographically and because Philip and Margaret Booth were there. I would come back later, twelve years later, in fact, with a new family and would eventually settle there.*"[21]

In addition to Josie, several other especially gifted Wellesley students developed their writing skills under Booth and became enduring friends of his: Kim Kurt (Waller), who studied with both Richard Wilbur and Philip Booth, placed poems in the *Hudson Review* after graduation and worked as a magazine features editor for *Mademoiselle* and *Town & Country.* Sue Ely, who became a private school teacher of English, later establishing an antiques business as well as becoming a nationally recognized breeder of Norfolk terriers, developed and sustained a rich forty-year correspondence with Booth—amazing by any standard; she visited the Booths in Maine almost every summer, making her way up Antiques Row from Wells to Kennebunk, acquiring pieces for her shop on her way to Castine. Gabrielle Ladd (Morss), who was equally skilled with pen, brush, and pencil, won the undergraduate poetry prize at Wellesley during her junior year and seemed destined for a career in the arts. But, like Josie Mankiewicz, she died tragically—in a plane crash at the age of twenty-three. In tribute to her talent, Booth arranged for a small privately printed collection of her poems, *The Dark Island: Twenty Poems*, writing the foreword himself.

It seems clear from the outset of Booth's teaching career that he habitually viewed his students as fellow travelers, embarked on their own journeys into the heart of the literature and poetry that spoke powerfully to them. Part of the effectiveness of his teaching was his willingness to identify and nurture the unique gifts his students brought to the conversation; his effect on his students was profound and enduring.

If the seven years in Lincoln had their joys—the birth of all three daughters; the adulation of a number of students who would become

Josie Mankiewicz Davis, upon the publication of her first novel, *Life Signs*, published in 1973, the year before her death.

lifelong friends; the rich tapestry of poets who lived and worked in the Boston area at that time, some of whom also became lifelong friends; the rigorous perspective of analysis; the rejuvenations of summers and holidays in Castine—there were also challenges.

Poets in the '50s and '60s were discovering the incalculable value of the reading circuit and routinely hit the road to read at colleges, universities, and libraries in the hope of attracting new readers and selling their books. For whatever reasons, Booth made a conscious decision not to give public readings. At times he explained that preparing for the reading siphoned off too much time, time better spent in writing and revising poems. On other occasions he admitted that his anxiety about travel and public speaking made the process a kind of torture. Stephen Dunn, the Pulitzer prize-winning poet who was a student of Booth's at Syracuse, observes, "I remember Phil telling me that he stopped giving public readings because they would make him nervous, and to prepare for them he'd often lose a week of writing time. I think that was initially true, but over time it became a part of his austere posture, a way of being. Puritans, of course, love to give things up. Not giving readings became a Philip Booth badge. I particularly regretted it because he was a fine reader. To hear him read (in person or on the phone) was to hear a form of punctuation. I have no doubt that if he had read in public as much as his contemporaries, his reputation would be greater now. I think if more people had heard Phil read, they'd hear the footsteps of a man walking through a town, talking to his neighbors as he went, the riffs and orchestration of asides, his own kind of jazz, no bopping or hijinks, but maybe like the Modern Jazz Quartet (his favorite)—a series of harmonies with a few dissonances thrown in. . . ."[22]

Maxine Kumin, who understood the importance of the reading circuit sufficiently to term it, wryly, Po-Biz, commented, "Phil was a carefully controlled person. It's a pity he never gave readings and it was an aspect of his anxiety that he could never quite master, despite the years of analysis. I know he would have liked to—because we talked about it—and of course it impeded his position in the hierarchy of poets; as we both knew, to get anywhere in Po-Biz you have to be out front and public. I shared with Phil my own strategies for combatting reading anxiety, since I, too, waged that battle, for years—imagining my mother's disapproving voice in the audience. I told him to read first a poem that was very short and light-hearted. And that if he didn't have one, to write one to use specifically at the beginning of a reading. When the audience laughs, you have time to collect yourself and then it is easier. But I guess it never got any easier for Phil."[23]

Despite an enthusiastic response from his students, and despite praise from friends like Peter Davis and colleagues like Richard Wilbur who saw him in action in the classroom, Wellesley did not offer Booth tenure. Wilbur, who a year earlier had left Wellesley for Wesleyan University, remembers their time together as young teaching colleagues. "Phil was a devoted teacher of undergraduate poetry writing," he says, "caring greatly about his students' efforts to find themselves. In his sympathy and fostering solicitude, he was much more involved than most writing teachers are."[24]

Syracuse University, however, was eager to recruit a poet of his caliber who also brought skill and dedication to the classroom. The university invited Booth to teach graduate writing courses in the fall of 1960, with an eye toward developing a graduate writing program at the university. He taught at Syracuse for the next two decades, cofounding the creative writing program, while gradually finding ways to free more and more time for writing in Castine. At Syracuse, in conjunction with Donald Justice, W. D. Snodgrass, and George P. Elliott, he taught young and hugely gifted poets like Stephen Dunn, Carol Frost, Jay Meek, and Larry Levis to "Be / careless of nothing. See / what you see."

The Syracuse years and their accompanying Castine summers were flourishing ones, a time of productive artistic work and deepening personal friendships. With his apprentice work behind him, he published, during those years, collections of poems every four or five years, voyaging more and more deeply into his emotional landscape: *The Islanders* (1961), *Weathers and Edges* (1966), *Margins* (1970), *Available Light* (1976), and *Before Sleep* (1980). Critical attention arrived in the form of reviews, literary prizes, and fellowships from the Guggenheim Foundation (two awards within six years) and the Rockefeller Foundation (1968). He liked the double rhythm of teaching at Syracuse and living for long stretches in Castine, since "each provided an escape route to another life." And some of the personal darkness he had fought in his Wellesley years receded. In a letter to Sue Ely dated September 21, 1968, he wrote, "The opportunity is mine to recognize that one's terrors and doubts and joys—however uniquely experienced—are finally not unique. Then one joins the human race."

That larger awareness of universal connectivity prompted renewed efforts to "let more and more into the poem." As he told Rachel Berghash, "I don't see myself as a localist in the sense of being provincial, in saying that this is the way it is in *this* place," but rather "that this is the way it is with being human in most places." Although the particulars of his poems derived largely from life on the coast of Maine, he worked to avoid being narrowly place-specific. If his distant kin Thoreau had "traveled much in Concord," so, too, Booth wished to travel much in Castine.

Not to Tell Lies

One of the most important friendships that Philip Booth made during the Boston "surge" years was with Robert Lowell, thanks again to the introductions of John Holmes. Their initial meeting was a case of comic misidentification, in fact. Booth remembered it this way:

> *My first year downcountry, driving John Holmes back from the Gardner house in Brookline, where we've been invited to meet Robert Lowell. The party is as big as the house, as casually elegant, to honor his homing from Iowa.*
>
> *As we drive back across the river, John asks what I thought about Lowell. Isabella Gardner I met, yes; Donald Hall, yes; and more poets than I ever knew existed. But I have to tell John I didn't meet Robert Lowell. I would have remembered that sternly handsome young man peering down from the gallery of*

The Robert Lowell that, initially, Booth
"somehow missed meeting."

> *portraits in Oscar Williams' newest anthology. No, I somehow missed meeting him. But as I tell John, I did have a good talk with another Lowell about his coming to Maine—a great bear of a man with hornrimmed glasses who slumped darkly away from me in a tall Victorian chair.*
>
> *"He must have been Lowell's brother," I tell John; "he said his name was Cal."*[1]

Although Booth met Lowell on several other occasions and attended many of the same readings and parties that brought the Boston group of poets together, it was Lowell's presence in Castine that cemented their friendship.

Harriet Winslow, an elderly cousin of Lowell's, was a summer resident of Castine. Starting in 1955, Lowell began visiting Castine every summer; when age prevented Harriet from summering there any longer, she willed the house to him. One June morning in 1957, Booth was pleasantly surprised to find Lowell collecting his mail at the Castine post office. Their friendship grew quickly, each admiring and needing some of the qualities of mind and heart that the other possessed.[2]

By the late 1950s, Robert "Cal" Lowell was considered one of the most gifted American poets of the twentieth century. He had achieved fame early when his second collection of poems, *Lord Weary's Castle*, won the Pulitzer Prize in 1947 when he was just thirty years old. A restless experimenter with multiple poetic forms, a public figure who traveled constantly to give readings and lectures, a translator, librettist, and teacher, Lowell led an often turbulent life interrupted by severe episodes of manic depression, often requiring hospitalization. The agonies of these episodes and their relentless frequency register in the letters and journals of many friends who loved and admired him, including those of Philip Booth.[3]

Lowell married Elizabeth "Lizzie" Hardwick in 1949. Born in

Steaming clams at Dyce Head Lighthouse, 1959: starting in the left foreground and moving clockwise are Margaret Booth, artist Clark Fitz-Gerald, Philip Booth, Robert Lowell, Elizabeth Hardwick, and Leah Fitz-Gerald.

Mary McCarthy, "just over the hedge."

Kentucky with the lifelong ambition to become "a New York Jewish intellectual," Hardwick achieved every part of that definition save the "Jewish." A critic, novelist, and essayist, she came to New York to work at the *Partisan Review*, where she met and was befriended by Philip Rahv, a bona fide New York Jewish intellectual. Later, she cofounded *The New York Review of Books,* which reshaped the intention, depth, and scope of the literary essay. In her role as a reviewer, Hardwick admired and accordingly praised Mary McCarthy's groundbreaking novels, essays, and criticism. She saw McCarthy's work as "an act of courage," arguing that "a career of candor and dissent is not an easy one for a woman."

Mary McCarthy's fame grew following the publication of the memoir *Memories of a Catholic Girlhood* (1957) and the novel *The Group* (1963).

But ultimately she was to make her mark as an acerbic critic on subjects cultural, literary, and political. As a critic, she could wield a scalpel like no other. Despite McCarthy's imperious reputation, Margaret Booth maintains that the person who lived right next door with her husband, former government diplomat James West, "was a warm and cordial person." McCarthy and West, married in 1961, bought the handsome Federalist-style house next to the Booths in 1967, partly at Hardwick's urging. McCarthy painted it yellow and set about creating in its gracious spaces the kind of literary salon she had enjoyed in Truro, on Cape Cod, some years earlier. West and McCarthy kept an apartment in Paris and spent summers in Castine for many years.

As this quartet of writers living in Castine's village orbit became close personal friends, they found enjoyment and stimulation in what one or another was reading or writing, or who was coming to visit, or what new ideas were in the air. For Philip Booth, the electric connection was with Cal Lowell, and when Lowell invited Booth to share some of his poems, he accepted. Several days later he visited Lowell's little barn/writing studio, set on the edge of a cove looking out into Castine Harbor, and listened intently as Lowell described his reactions to the poems. Later, in his journal, he wrote: "I begin to understand that I am for the first time hearing a master teacher. I listen and listen, reminding myself that when I get home I must write myself notes about everything Cal is saying. . . . Nobody before has ever cared to criticize them so brilliantly, cared to demand of them, even in parts so cared to praise them, as Cal has done this day."[4]

If Lowell was a poet he could entrust with his poems, Booth could reveal to Lowell an insider's understanding of Castine, its history, its nautical lore, its language and voice. Lowell was fascinated, and hungrily pressed Booth to take him sailing and tell him stories in "his Maine voice." Booth agreed, though quietly observing in his journal, "In matters practical, Cal has no native talent."

Margaret remembers summers with "this extraordinarily talented group of friends" in this way:

> *At first, it was a little daunting to have Mary McCarthy right over the hedge. By that time Philip had determined that he was going*

to be a writer; his close relationship with Robert Frost had really set him on his life's path. So to have this collection of talented writers converging, summer after summer, in Castine was not only exciting, it was enriching. Mary McCarthy became a great friend of Philip's. They exchanged many books and talked about them enthusiastically; her dinner parties were famous and we were fortunate to be included in many.

I was especially fond of Lizzie. She was a southerner, was from Kentucky, so we immediately had common ground. She and Cal had not only the house on the common, the Harriet Winslow house, but also a barn on the waterfront that Cal converted to his studio. Philip spent many hours there talking poetry. Lizzie and Cal entertained all sorts of artists and writers—and even political figures like Ted Kennedy and Gene McCarthy. We were included in many of these gatherings and they were fascinating evenings of good talk and high spirits.

Cal especially appreciated Philip's skill in telling Maine stories—and indeed he could sound like a true Mainer—in the pace and rhythm of the story, the inflections, the humor. He never told Maine stories in a patronizing way, for he was absolutely devoted to Castine.

He had such a long history in Castine, and I think that is, in part, what fascinated Cal. He had spent every summer there from the time he was a little boy; by the time he was ten or twelve, he had a little boat. As the story goes, one summer a Chinese vessel came into the harbor and this little boat was among the things aboard. When the vessel left, the little boat stayed with Philip. It was always tied up at Dennett's Wharf where Joe and Jake Dennett, and before them their boatbuilder father, looked after the sailboats of many of the local sailors. Philip was allowed to take the boat out on his own—and so on many days he'd saunter down to the wharf, ready to go for a sail. Jake would look up the hill and see him coming. Then he'd look up to the sky, he'd test the wind, and he'd look at the outlet. So by the time Philip got there he'd be able to say, "Yup, you can go out," or "Not today,

Lowell, Booth, their families and friends, launched on a picnic sailing trip.

Philip." Cal loved hearing about recollections like this one and took special delight in stories that underscored the warm and loyal bonds native Castiners had with one another. That's part of what made his breakdowns so sad—since he pushed people away and alienated others because of his turmoil. His illnesses made life difficult for Lizzie, though she persevered for a long time. Being married to Robert Lowell could not have been an easy task."[5]

As prescient as Margaret's understated final sentence is, what lingers in Booth's descriptions of his friendship with Cal Lowell is the magnetic force of his personality and intellect.

The Ram Island picnic excursion, 1967.

People come to talk with Cal, to listen to how his brilliance works. What's remarkable is how steadily, even with visitors, Cal keeps to his writing routine. Almost daily, Cal's day moves from the old isolations of poems to the strong refreshment of people. Breakfast, post office, Barn; work and lunch, until it is time for tennis and people again. People come to talk with Cal; they also come to share in Elizabeth's brilliance, to share her table, to be part of her house. And part of the idea of summer. Almost the only exception to Cal's working schedule is dictated by that alchemy of people and weather which turns a day into a picnic.

We used to go to Ram Island, mostly by way of a couple of outboard-powered rowboats, and by ferrying people on our small sloop. This year, perhaps because the picnics have been considerably enlarged by the arrival of Mary McCarthy and Jim West and their household, from Paris, we've gone to Smith's Mill—a millrace cover with a clamshell beach that lies three miles across the harbor from Cal's Barn.

Over breakfast, the weather comes clear. Mary and Elizabeth, by phone, start collecting people and salads; and, beyond outboard and sail power, a lobsterboat hired from Eaton's Wharf. We all gather there at eleven, and begin to meet each other's visitors. By the time we're all ashore again at Smith's Mill, dinghy-load after dinghy-load, I figure that this has become the picnic to end all picnics. Years ago, I came here with an aged aunt or boys my own age, to eat jelly sandwiches and dig for arrowheads in the shellheap bank above the shell beach. Today there are over twenty people picnicking by the millrace. To name them, to say the languages being spoken in this mostly lonely cove, is to suggest how much of the world, and what parts of it have gravitated here—and primarily because of Cal.

Harris and Mary Thomas, from Exeter, are talking in French about their memory of Rennes with the newest addition to our crew: an AFS student just arrived from Brittany. Priscilla Barnum is with Margaret and Elizabeth, who trade Georgia talk for Kentucky talk between tending fire and attending to daughters. Margot, our seventeen-year-old Bikini, is putting her high school Russian to the test, listening to Olga Carlisle explaining some nuances of Pasternak's to Cal. As I take some photographs of all this, I have just had it explained to me, by a Classics professor from Cincinnati that xai ov, the name of our dinghy, is badly spelled Greek. Henry Carlisle is talking American English to Sonia Orwell, whose English is British; Ted Draper and James West have given up on Sonia's conversation and have turned their mutual interest to Poland. Jim, in Polish, asks something of Maria, whom he and Mary have imported from their Paris apartment to serve their establishment here. Native Pole though she is, Maria answers in French; she is helping Jim's sons, Johnny and Danny, dig for flints on the bank above us. Robin and Harriet are huddled in towels on opposite sides of the fire after a quick duck in the local edge of the Labrador current. Carol, our almost-sixteen, has stayed in longer than anybody except Mary McCarthy—who, since coming to Castine has become, by general acclaim, the Champion Stayer-In-Of-All-Time. As Mary and Carol stroke slowly toward the shore, Margot comes up to me in full amazement, and speaks (though she does not know it) in that same daughterly voice Thomas Wolfe once heard at his editor's breakfast table:

"Daaaddy, do you know how many languages people are talking here?"

I assent to her amazement.

"You know," she says, "if some Mohawks or Penobscots, or whoever they'd be, crawled out of that shellheap, somebody here could probably talk Indian to them . . . "

Who, for instance?

Her eyes slide down the shell beach toward Cal in his L. L. Bean red shirt, his hands gesticulating wildly. "Well," she hesitates, "probably Mr. Lowell."[6]

~

Despite his prodigious talent, Cal Lowell wasn't the only "master teacher" in Castine during those years. Although he might have been the last person to apply this title to himself, Philip Booth was presiding over a new crop of talented writers at Syracuse each year, each of whom was attempting to discern his own poetic voice, his own way of discovering "how words see." Stephen Dunn described what it was like to be in a Philip Booth classroom:

> *I've had a lot of luck in my life, but certainly among the luckiest was finding myself in Philip's workshop at Syracuse in 1969. There was this impressive-looking, quite formal man who, on the first day of class introduced us to each other, never asking for our input. He had done his homework about our pasts, and referred to each of us as, say, Mr. Dunn or Mr. Levis. "Mr. Dunn is a graduate of Hofstra*

and comes to us from New York City via the corporate world, and lately from a year of living in Spain. Mr. Levis is from Fresno, California, and studied with Philip Levine and Robert Mezey," and so on until all seven of us were sketched. Remember, this was 1969, when formalities were under fire as were most semblances of authority. In a sense, he was introducing us to who he was, and when he spoke about our poems it was a further introduction to his character and principles. Though he was open to a variety of styles, he was not open to anything that smacked of posturing or easy cleverness, or any form of disingenuousness. He had not yet written his wonderful poem "Not to Tell Lies," but he was, in effect, the embodiment of it. One of the most important lessons that Philip taught—without overtly teaching it—was that writing poetry was not "creative writing"; it was an extension of one's life, a way of exploring what it felt like to be alive in one's body in a certain place at a certain time.

I never heard him refer to his mentor, Robert Frost, as other than Mr. Frost. I was acutely aware of this, which deterred me from calling him Philip for many years. I think I was in my early 40s before I ventured to call him Philip. In those years between 1969 and, say, 1980, when our relationship was moving toward friendship, I don't know what I called him, not Mr. Booth, but probably, "Hello," or "Hi"; those were his names. Nor did he give me permission to call him Philip. My guess is that he rather liked my little dance around the issue of boundaries, yet probably was pleased when I could finally call him by his first name. I mention this because he was a man of very defined boundaries.

For example, in my second year at Syracuse, my then-wife and I felt very honored to be invited to his house for drinks before dinner. I remember exactly how he framed the invitation: "Why don't you come around 4:30 and leave at a quarter to six." Philip was wonderful company when he knew the social parameters in advance, somewhat fidgety company when he didn't. Of course he had the great fortune of having Margaret for a wife. A man could afford a number of eccentricities if he had Margaret to carry the day. I suspect Philip learned this early, and it became one of the factors in the freedom he felt in being selves rather than just self. Self was firmly rooted; the selves he placed under the scrutiny of the unsparing language of his poems. Margaret, his children, and Castine were the anchors—everything else was adrift. His poems, especially the ones from mid-career on, sought to find words for that elusiveness. They are important poems; they echo the intensity of their making, they testify to a long war between

A party in honor of Donald Justice drew these members of the Syracuse Writing Program Faculty in June 1970: Philip Booth, George Elliott, W. D. Snodgrass, Donald Justice, Donald Dike.

Members of Booth's writing seminar at Syracuse gathered for a picnic and bonfire November 1969. Stephen Dunn is to the right of the horse; Larry Levis is next to Booth, who is piling on the brush.

> *passion and restraint, a war that was constantly being lost and won. He seemed amused by the ambiguities and paradoxes that resulted. That is, when he wasn't being tormented by them."*[7]

Dunn recalled who, in his estimation, was the most talented poet to emerge from that group: Larry Levis, who, after a brilliant and all too brief career, died of a heart attack at the age of forty-nine.

> *We had come to study with Philip Booth, Donald Justice, W. D. Snodgrass, George P. Elliott, arguably the best group of writer-teachers that existed at the time. In Philip Booth's small workshop that first semester in 1969, I kept silent most of the time. There was a very brilliant Fellowship student (I'll not name him) from the South who held forth every class. None of us was articulate, certainly not Larry whose speech was hesitant, at worst sprinkled*

> *with "you knows," a kind of punctuation for him, sometimes annoying, like "like" these days. The brilliant student's poems, however, were convoluted. We soon learned that his brilliance, his apparent brilliance, was overly convoluted too. Much elaboration and ranginess, little touching down. In a month or so, it was clear who was the most interesting and able poet. Booth clearly knew. When that year Larry won The Academy of American Poets Award for best poem, no one was surprised.* [8]

Musician Lou Reed, later known for his 1970s hit "Walk on the Wild Side," was also a student of Booth's—and was in the process of carving out a considerable reputation for the brooding, urban, and poetic content of his songs. "I wasn't a very useful teacher for him," Booth observed, "because he already had an ear for the kind of songs he'd later write. But he was a very interesting young poet."[9]

Schooled by his experiences at Wellesley when teaching and advising responsibilities left scant time for his own work, Booth began to build into his teaching schedule at Syracuse little oases of time that he could use to refine and deepen the possibilities in his own poetry. At first, the family spent the entire school year in Syracuse and the summer months in Castine. But gradually he began to cluster his courses into one semester, stretching from January to May, freeing time for writing during the summer, which then flowed seamlessly into the fall months. Eventually he and Margaret sold the house on North Eagle Village Road in Manlius, renting an apartment in Syracuse in its place, signaling that the Castine house would, when finances permitted, become their permanent home. By 1986 they moved to Castine, where they remained until 2002, when Booth's declining health required a transfer to a retirement community in Hanover.

Winters in upstate New York were as challenging as winters in Castine, and the Booth daughters remember their junior high and high school years as dominated by white expanses of snow—removed, more or less successfully, with a snow plow attached to a WWII jeep their father maintained. But it was early spring that brought one of Robin Booth's most memorable experiences.

> *I was maybe thirteen or so and out at the end of our driveway waiting for a ride to some event or another. Suddenly, while I was waiting, I heard a piercing cry for help. I heard it several times, persistent and haunting, with silence in the intervals. I walked back to the house to tell Dad and he came out to stand with me. Unmistakably, there was the cry again, "Help"; and so we went out, gathering a few others in small groups, little posses really, to search for who was sending that distress call. It turned out that the distressed caller was a peacock who lived with nearby neighbors who had a collection of exotic birds. The peacock's cry is unnervingly close to a human's cry for help. After we disbanded in relief and laughter and went on our separate ways, I thought about my dad's reaction: I was grateful he had taken me seriously and helped me investigate if anybody was in danger. He cared—and that counted.*[10]

During the first years of teaching at Syracuse, Booth appeared to be engaged in assessing the role of the teacher and what gifts he might bring to that vocation. In a February 1967 letter to Sue Ely, he wrote: "A teacher, at best, teaches, gives, whatever, from what, hopefully, is incentive-from-the-inside. He may, in some minor way, be directly rewarded by seeing a student come through with a good exam, a good paper, a good job. But that direct reward hardly signifies at all beside the rewards he seldom even knows, much less sees. . . . Melville, I think it was, spoke of the 'universal nudge' that passed around—perhaps on antarctic whaling voyages—that nudge, that bit of luck that the teacher once tried to give. But if the teacher teaches in the hope of direct return, his teaching is hardly teaching at all—but rather he's interposing himself into the act of sharing—asking for the sharing to come his way." Acutely aware of the costs as well as the rewards of teaching when one's primary vocation is writing, Booth sought to teach with passion and creativity, to assist in the development of a student's craft without depleting the creative energy that fueled his own work.

Striking the right balance for the writer-teacher is often a difficult task. Stephen Dunn, who also has spent many years as a college teacher, describes the struggle in this way:

> *Teaching is one kind of mastery, one way of knowing and becoming intimate with your subject. . . . I don't think it can hurt your writing as long as you remain more of a poet than a teacher. That's the difficult balance. When the scale tips toward teaching as your primary identity, when the struggles and pleasures of the classroom supersede the struggles and pleasures of the page, as can easily happen, that's when you must rightly call yourself a teacher, an honorable enough title to be sure, but a capitulation to safer territory in which a text already exists and there's no permanent record of what you said.*
>
> *It's no accident that more good poetry arises out of crises and dilemmas than out of triumph and jobs well done. We are less likely to confront self and world when we're satisfied with self and world. We're less likely to have that edge that leads to discovery. The poet must always be to some degree an outsider, must always be probing for what's hidden or unexplored, must always resist what passes for reality.*[11]

Philip Booth's natural inclination to see himself as "an outsider" served what Dunn would see as one of poetry's prime necessities. So, too, did his habit of returning to Castine—where his community included not only family and local friends, but an ambitious circle of writers who exercised rigorous discipline in creating and revising their own work.

Booth was especially devoted to revision. As Patrick Walker, Booth's former son-in-law and lifelong friend, remembers:

> *He would sit for hours at a time, refining versions of each poem. It was not unusual for poems to undergo 20–25 drafts. Often, after he had been working on a poem for some time, he'd read it to us at the dinner table, as if testing reactions to hearing its sound and shape aloud. Then he might go back upstairs and revise again. He was painstaking with language, with choosing exactly the right words that would release meaning.*[12]

His own revision process deepened his conviction that poetry was, or could be, a vehicle "not to tell lies." That boyhood revelation many years earlier (which dawned on him after reading Frost's "After Apple-Picking") became a central informing tenet in his poems.

> *We're subjected to so much lying from high places, we're bombarded by falsehood in the television; we're so emotionally assaulted by all of this, we so lightly lie to ourselves in our lesser and sometimes in our deeper relations, including our relations with ourselves, that there is a tremendous need for the poet to know that he or she is not—through whatever abstracting or fictionalizing—telling lies.*
>
> *"Not to Tell Lies" is, after all, about returning to this house [Castine] and writing in the back bedroom with my ancestors' portraits on the wall, with the rock a doctor brought me back from Amchitka . . . of all in this village that sustains me.* [13]

Rather than Lowell's restless experimentation, Booth decided to hold to his own emotional and geographical territory, mining it as deeply as he could.

His decision, however, did not prohibit new kinds of visual and auditory experimentation on the page. "Not to Tell Lies" is one example of such inventiveness. Instead of the narrow vertical "tower of words" poems that had been his structural thumbprint, Booth arranged the words of this poem in a kind of crescendo/decrescendo movement. The poem begins with the physical coordinates of his situation: age, location, physical space. These concrete specifics, in turn, trigger emotional, intellectual, and spiritual associations, which build into a contrapuntal interweaving of those things he holds dear, those things he can trust, on which he can depend. Their surging power offers assurance, then pulls back into quiet but intense *recitative*, capturing his credo, his this-I-believe.

Not to Tell Lies

He has come to a certain age.
To a tall house older than he is.
Older, by far, than he will ever be.
He has moved his things upstairs, to a room
which corners late sun. It warms a schooner model,
his daughter's portrait, the rock his doctor brought him
back from Amchitka. When he looks at the rock he thinks Melville;
when he touches the lichen he dreams Thoreau. Their testaments
shelve the inboard edge of the oak-legged table he writes on.
He has nailed an ancestor's photograph high over his head.
He has moored his bed perpendicular to the North wall;
whenever he rests his head is compassed barely west
of Polaris. He believes in powers: gravity, true
North, magnetic North, love. In how his wife
loved the year of their firstborn. Whenever he wakes he sees the clean page in
his portable. He has sorted life out;
he feels moved to say all of it,
most of it all. He tries
to come close, he keeps
coming close: he has
gathered himself
in order not
to tell
lies.

Two of Booth's best-known poems, "Eaton's Boatyard" and "Building Her," were written at about the same time as "Not to Tell Lies," and appear in the collection titled *Before Sleep.* The poems reveal the value of linking the particulars of a special location (the wharf area of the Castine harbor) or activity (the art of boatbuilding) to the universal effort of finding "what will suffice," the job of choosing and making and remaking, with whatever materials are available, the shape of a life, or an art. Once again, the poems offer versions of Booth's experiments with organicism: how they appear on the page or how they sound when read aloud contributes to what they mean. In "Eaton's Boatyard," the words are strewn around on the page like the culch strewn about on the boatyard floor; in "Building Her," Booth employs aural echoing and personification to explore how "wood works," how it "remembers," "shivers," "refuses," "binds," and "breathes." The form the poem takes and its meaning are inseparable.

The actual Eaton's Boatyard is located on Sea Street, situated, like Dennett's Wharf, at the hub of the Castine waterfront, backed by one of the most beautiful deep harbors on the East Coast. Philip knew the place intimately from the time he was a boy and knew well the three generations of Eatons who owned and ran the boatyard: Mace Eaton, a master boatbuilder, many of whose beautiful wooden craft are still in use today; his son, Alonzo, or Lon, who also built beautiful boats and who, with his father, is credited as the designer and builder of the Castine day-sailers still seen in and around Castine; and Ken, Lon's son, who currently owns and operates the boatyard. The three generations of Eatons appear often in Booth's photographs, and Booth was an active member of what was whimsically called the Wharf Historical Society, a group of townsfolk and sailors and fishermen who gathered several late afternoons a week at Dennett's Wharf to discuss matters of interest to them all.

"Eaton's Boatyard," by Booth's own account, sprang from retrieving certain words that carried a long history in waterfront boatyards: *culch, pulling-boat molds, potwarp.*

> *When I was maybe forty, still hanging around the waterfront, I heard a young boy yell to his father, Alonzo Eaton, "Dad, when're you going to clean up this christly culch?" I missed the ultimate word the first time he yelled, but I got him quieted down to say it again. And when I got back home to an unabridged dictionary, there it was: a word so old that Cabot or Champlain may have imported it to my home coast, a word I trust is as self-explanatory in the context of the poem as it was when the boy first yelled it.*
>
> *Culch may be, in the poem, more self-evident than potwarp*

"Culch" inside Eaton's Boatyard, most easily translated as "junk with a purpose."

(the kind of line that attaches a lobsterman's buoy to his trap far below), or pulling boat-molds (the wooden patterns around which old Maine rowboats were built.")[14]

But clearly, Booth's love of words, especially those that transport the reader to another world in time, one still embedded in the present, was a trigger for his imagination. "My father," says Carol Booth, "adored words like *culch*, which could most easily be translated as "junk with a purpose." To him it meant so much more and could lead him down a road—into the heart of a poem." As Booth himself said, "Even in the culch of Eaton's Boatyard or the apparent chaos of being alive, nothing is ever lost."[15]

Eaton's Boatyard

To make do, make a living:
to throw away nothing,
practically nothing, nothing that may
come in handy;
within an inertia of caked paintcans,
frozen C-clamps, blown strips of tarp, and
pulling-boat molds,
to be able to find,
for whatever it's worth,
what has to be there:
the requisite tool
in this culch there's no end to:
the drawshave buried in potwarp,
chain, and manila jibsheets,
or, under the bench,
the piece that already may fit
the idea it begins
to shape up:
not to be put off by split rudders,
stripped outboards, half
a gasket, and nailsick garboards:
to forget for good
all the old year's losses,
save for
what needs to be retrieved:
a life given to
how today feels:
to make of what's here
what has to be made
to make do.

Lon Eaton, master boat builder; the portrait was taken by Rollie McKenna, who became famous for her photographs of poets and artists in the '50s and '60s. She came to Castine frequently, photographing Booth, Lowell, and the Eatons on several occasions.

Three generations of Eatons: Mace, Kenny, Lon, summer of 1969.

"Building Her," at least in its particulars, describes Booth's own early experience in woodworking, as well as his lifelong love of small sailing vessels, several of the most graceful of which were designed and built by Mace and Lon Eaton. As the boatbuilder fashions his vessel, so, the poem implies, the poet pares away anything that is ornamental in his craft—to get at an essence. "That starkness," Booth observed, "is for me a way to let objects or emotions illuminate themselves."[16]

Building Her

Wood: learning it:
feeling the tree
shiver the helve, feeling the grain
resist the saw, feeling for grain
with adze and chisel, feeling the plank
refuse a plane, the voyage of sap
still live in the fiber;
joining wood:
scarfing it, rabbeting keel and sternpost,
matching a bevel, butting a joint
or driving a trunnel:
whatever fastens
the grain, the grain lets in, and binds;

let wood breathe or keep wood briny,
wood will outlive generations:

working wood, a man learns how
wood works:
wood comes and goes
with weather or waves; wood gives:

come to find right grain for timbers,
keelson, stem, a man can feel
how wood remembers:
the hull will
take to sea the way the tree knew wind.

Booth was consciously exploring ways to vary the shape and line lengths he employed in poems. As he observed some years later, "I used to be inclined to do what one of my students, Larry Levis, called "tuck the poem under at the end." I'm now inclined to leave it more open-ended, more ambivalent."[17] As he moved away from "word towers" or strictly controlled stanzas, the techniques he used in his poems began to resemble the craft of the boatbuilders he so admired—carving out the shape stroke by stroke, form following function.

Booth's fascination with boats and boatbuilding, though reinforced by living in the sea-saturated atmosphere of Castine, was not something he learned from his father or mother, or even inherited from his grandparents. His father's parents were Midwesterners, and while his mother and grandmother spent many years in Castine, they were not, in Patrick Walker's phrase, "sea people." It was Philip who loved the water, who, after acquiring "his own little boat," aspired to own a real sailboat and learn to sail with the skill that a good boat merited. He took some lessons at the Castine Yacht Club, read about boats, practiced on his own, talked with the sailors who gathered almost every day during the summer months on the wharf, and, as he had always hoped, came to own a succession of boats—all clearly well loved and well documented in photographs; he, in turn, taught Margaret to sail and then each of his young daughters. As Carol remembers:

> *The first of my family's sailboats that I remember was the Little Myth. During the time we had that boat, we also had a little dinghy that my father built for the three of us to learn how to row in; it was appropriately called Little Sis (and it still lives in the garage in Castine). We had a sailboat somewhat later called Xaipe, and a Castine day-sailer sloop, the class of boat built by Mace Eaton, called Alar. Somewhere in there we had a Boston Whaler named Hval, which I think means "whale" in some Scandinavian language. And finally we had Festina, a very pretty sailboat, which was accompanied by a dinghy Dad christened Lente. Growing up, we spent hours and hours on the water in one or another of these boats.*

Carol and Robin told very similar stories about the naming of the boats and the way their father rigged the process. As Carol puts it, "The naming of a new boat always became a huge procedure in my father's mind; names were solicited, opinions were discussed, possibilities were compared. Gradually it dawned on us that our father had worn us all down deliberately—in order to choose his own entry. It became a family joke."[18]

~

Castine, in the decades Philip taught at Syracuse, continued to simmer with artists and writers. Mary McCarthy and Jim West continued to summer next door to the Booths, and during the '60s Cal Lowell and Lizzie Hardwick, with their young daughter, Harriet, spent considerable periods of time there, though Lowell was increasingly active politically, protesting the Vietnam War in a variety of forums and, in 1968, offering public support for Eugene McCarthy's candidacy for president. Although Lowell continued writing in a variety of media—plays, librettos, poems, translations—nothing could entirely moderate the wide swings between manic and depressive episodes. In the '50s, thorazine had been thought to be the wonder drug that would stabilize him; lithium arrived a decade later, but it, too, was only marginally effective.

A younger group of writers began to explore the joys of Castine summer living, among them Peter Davis, who returned twelve years after losing Josie, this time with his second wife, Karen Zehring, and their two young children. As Peter recalls:

> *I came to see the Booths following a camping trip on Mount Desert Island in Acadia National Park. Our children were very young, but this was a lovely family camp, complete with cots and tents and planned activities; we had a marvelous time. We came over to visit with the Booths, who in the interim had become friends. It was a friendship based not simply on the fact that Philip had been Josie's teacher, but on our delight in coming to know Margaret, Philip's wife. We were absolutely enamored of Margaret; the two were a wonderful couple.*
>
> *We repeated that camping trip a second time and during that second visit [to Castine] decided to look at houses. I spotted this 1782 house from the realtor's waterfront office. When I saw the Palladian window on the second floor, I fell in love. It took some time to restore the house, but it was well worth the effort.*
>
> *In fact, before I remarried, I visited with a girlfriend whom Philip liked enormously. This young woman must have felt, or so I believe as I look back on it, overwhelmed by all the memories*

Carol Allen, sailing in Castine in the early '70s.

of Josie that automatically came her way. Josie was such a free spirit and so memorable that people couldn't help talking about her; probably those memories, true though they were, were hard to hear over and over again. She was very aware that she was coming into my life after the tragedy of Josie's early death. Philip was sensitive to the shadow that hung heavily on this young woman, and during that visit he took us out to a plot of land they owned on the coast to watch silently as the sun set. It was a beautiful moment. And Phil said, "The sun, as it sets, leaves a lovely glow, but it casts no shadow." She got the metaphor.

Karen, my wife, loved to play Charades; that game, you probably remember, was wildly popular in the '70s. Each person draws a card that has a phrase or saying or place on it and then acts out, without speaking, clues that help the others guess the word. I remember one particular time when we were playing with Phil and Margaret, who acted as a team. Phil, the "word man," could be deadly effective in this game. They chose their word, left the room, and returned exhibiting this behavior: each of them would place a hand on someone's brow, or open someone's mouth and peer in, or listen to the chest as if with a pretend stethoscope, always working in tandem. We all guessed and guessed to no avail. Finally they revealed what they were acting out: pair-o-docs, or paradox. We all laughed and laughed.[19]

Carol Allen, who with her husband, Bob, enjoyed a sixty-year close friendship with the Booths, offered additional glimpses of the spontaneous and fun-loving side of a man so often characterized as reserved and "a man of boundaries." Bob Allen was an undergraduate at Dartmouth at the same time Booth entered college; he left during WWII and returned after his military service to graduate. He, too, went to New York, to Columbia for a master's degree in English, the same year that Philip and Margaret were in New York. During the '50s while the Booths were in Lincoln with their young girls, the Allens lived nearby with their growing family and visited often "that wonderful little house in Lincoln set in the middle of apple orchards." In fact, Carol Allen described their long friendship as one riding "on parallel paths," so perhaps it was not surprising that the Allens, after visiting in Castine for a number of summers, decided to build a house there.

Bob and Philip together made a terrific pair; they had complementary senses of humor, they both loved words—and were good with them—and they loved to sing. Philip, in particular, loved to dance. One time when we were visiting in Castine, there was a major party on the big ship, the State of Maine, anchored in the harbor. Even though we hadn't been invited, we all wanted to go. Philip just waved his hands dismissively, saying, "I know the Captain; it will be okay." So off we went to the dance and had a great time. You could say we all got "quite happy." On the way home we stopped at the Castine Inn, and Philip and Bob sat on the front steps and sang a whole medley of Frank Sinatra songs and show tunes—much to the delight of the patrons of the inn.

Bob and Philip also had a special fascination with Sophia Loren. She was all the rage in the movies then, and they found her ravishing. Well, one summer we rented a house in Castine for a month. When we drove up to the house, Sophia Loren was posted on the front door. Philip had found a photo in Vanity Fair and had enlarged it for Bob's enjoyment.[20]

Booth's love of sailing continued unabated: in addition to taking friends and family on various excursions, he occasionally taught young novices the rudiments of sailing. One such sailor, Henry Miller, remembers a Booth lesson that extended beyond simple navigational tactics:

I learned of Philip Booth's love of the Maine coast firsthand, when he agreed many summers ago to teach a group of five promising teenage sailors in Castine the advanced skills needed for successful sailing along the Maine coast. We studied diligently and enthusiastically, and, when the course was complete, he flunked us all. Our failing was not that we weren't technically proficient (we really were quite good); he failed us because we weren't "observant enough."

During the final exam, he had unrolled a chart of Penobscot Bay (Chart 1203, to be exact) and had pointed to two spots on the coast. "If you were surrounded by fog, and the fog lifted here and here," he had asked, pointing twice, "what would you see?" None of us knew. (The correct answers were: an osprey nest and a large-windowed porch on a house perched on a cliff).

Strangely, despite our effort, none of us minded or protested. He was setting a high standard and challenging us to reach it, knowing that we could. He was saying that to be a truly good sailor you not only had to master the skills of sailing but demonstrate a keen appreciation of your surroundings. He had so much respect for the coast—its beauty and its sometimes unforgiving elements—that he wouldn't accredit us until we learned to appreciate it just as much.

> *Late that summer, after a successful two-day sail in what became some particularly difficult weather, he announced that we had all passed and would not have to take the test again. We had learned our lesson, and it had changed how we all looked at the coast.*[21]

Robert Lowell was the friend who most pressed Booth to take him on sailing adventures. Lowell's exuberance and clumsiness, at least in executing skills that required coordination and grace—such as sailing or tennis—were subjects Booth mocked gently in his essay "Robert Lowell's Summers in Castine."

> *Against sunset, against summer's end, against the prevailing sou-westerlies which stress and release even the peninsula's strongest elms, Cal plays tennis almost every afternoon at one of the two courts next to the High Road. The company at these late-afternoon sessions of round-robin doubles is socially elect. The voices are pure Eastern Shore, West Hartford, and Boston, but the talent is severely mixed; Cal wins one set with Janet Hughes, twenty years his senior, then loses a second set with Sally Austin, skilled and barely of age. His legs never get him to the right place on the court at the right moment, but he compensates by attacking the ball with all the immense strength of his upper body. His reflexes, if not always coordinated, are quick: even when his stroke flails he scores points with his running monologue—this particular game variously reminds him of Philip of Macedonia, his first wife, and Aristophanes. Elizabeth, exhausted after two sets, gangles on the sidelines under the cedars.*
>
> *Cal is about to serve. Sweating hugely, he strips off his shirt (violating the only club rule ever posted), and says, "This may make me as famous as René Lacoste. . . ." Wherever fame may reside, it will not reside in his service: he throws that ball too low, ducks from his knees to accommodate the failed altitude, pushes at the ball from too short an arc, and with great speed squashes it into his partner's left buttock. She smiles back wildly at Cal, and he invites everybody for supper.*

Cal is not the only participant subject to Booth's withering eye, however:

> *Cal wanted to be taken out sailing; Margaret and I obliged by taking him out around the bell. As we came back into the harbor on a dying breeze, I asked Cal if he wanted to take the helm. He did, accompanied by improbable tales of his sailing in Padanaram as a boy. These somehow slid into a wonderfully funny story about sexual mores in Dubuque; a wonderfully funny story at which Margaret laughed more than I only because Cal was letting the boat gybe at will, all over the harbor. The air was too light to have these gyrations hurt the boat, but she was easily identifiable along the waterfront, and it hurt my pride to have her sailed so badly in such public view. Aside from some suggestions, readily accepted by Cal, to head for this buoy, or that farm on the shore, I held in my frustration until we neared the wharves. I mentioned the difficult set of the current, took back the helm from Cal, and buttonhooked up to our mooring. Margaret neatly picked up the pennant with the boathook, but then proceeded to cleat it with perhaps her right hand rather than her left. I jumped forward past Cal with all my frustration vented on my wife, grabbed the pennant from her, cleated it the other way around, and stood quickly straight up, puffing angrily on my pipe. Next thing I knew I stepped one step smartly backwards, plunk into the harbor.*[22]

If Cal could be the target and instigator of comic relief, his brilliant talk and careful reading of Booth's poems more than compensated for some of the demands of being his friend. As Booth acknowledged in several ways in both essays and poems, "Cal is like an archeologist at the dig-site; there are ages and ages under him. . . . I don't know anybody who has felt as much, who has thought as deeply."[23]

Nowhere was this more evident than when the Kennedys sailed into Castine's harbor in the late summer of 1965. As Booth recalled:

> *Cruising sailors often think of this as a good fogport, and we're fairly used to having old friends descend on us by boat in foul weather. But this August morning, in ample sun, we got a phone call from an acquaintance on North Haven, asking if we could*

The beautifully renovated great room that stands at a right angle to 95 Main Street. Called by the Booths simply The Shed in honor of its origins, it was in front of this towering fireplace that Lowell, the Booths, the Kennedys, and their entourage had their evening of electric conversation.

take care of the friends who are chartering his boat. My father is visiting, Robin's in bed with the flu on this ninth birthday of hers; I was much relieved to find that Margaret and I were only being asked to locate rooms ashore for the charter party and, if possible, to meet them at the wharf when they made port. Then I got told who the charterers were, and how many; they took all the available rooms in the town's one inn.

I'm not used to Kennedys, even junior senators from Massachusetts, much less a whole Washington caucus of Kennedy friends. But they seemed pleased to be met at the wharf when they sailed in casually late; they were grateful for our having found rooms for them; and, yes, they'd love the ten-minute tour of the town on the way to the inn. Places where history and revolution happened: the promontory where the French first landed thirteen years before Plymouth, the British fort that frightened Saltonstall into losing his fleet, the Paul Revere bell in the tower of the Unitarian Church—all these interest them. Turning by the church, I point out the house that quartered British officers in 1812; and here, on the opposite corner of the common, the house where the poet Robert Lowell lives. They might know that just this June, as an act of protest against our involvement in Vietnam, he refused President Johnson's invitation to the White House. They do know. Could they meet him? I offer our Shed, and drinks if that wouldn't interfere with their plans. . . .

In due time everybody arrives at the summer living room at the ell-end of our house. . . . John Tunney and John Culver and Ted Kennedy want to hear from Cal why he turned down the President. They do hear.

Talk gathers momentum though the drinking is slow. I am only on the edge of it, moving around to pass drinks and cheese, going to and from the kitchen. By the sink, Margaret and I exchange impressions; beyond liking Joan immediately, we find we're similarly astonished: these are the people who are running the country, and "they're all younger than we are."

But age is not why they defer to Cal. And as I tend the logs my father has lit in the big stone fireplace, I realize that what started as a casual symposium has mostly turned into a dialogue. Cal is at the fireplace end of the couch, Marieve Rugo and Mieke Tunney beside him, across from the big window looking out into fields. The others are variously spread round the room: in wicker chairs, on the bookcase under the window, on the floor by the fire. Just across a low bench from Cal is Ted, sitting in a ladderback chair, and leaning forward as far as his backbrace will allow. And he is conducting what has become a kind of subcommittee hearing, question after question being put to the expert witness.

Cal's grasp of politics is new to me, or newly marvelous. Out of nowhere, making analogues from his trip to Brazil, he begins naming South American names, and coming up with figures on income and distribution—figures which sound more like a Kennedy than a Cal. But the hands are Cal's, intensely moving, and so is the voice: a Beacon Hill nasality, varying always in pitch no matter how low the volume. As I go for drinks I catch only snatches:

"I didn't want to lend even tacit approval to what he's begun to do to us."

"I don't know what to do about it, Senator; that's up to you." His hand includes Iowa and California. "What I do know is that what we're doing in Vietnam is only more terrible, and more visible, than what we're probably doing in Chile. Or what we've already done in Santo Domingo."

"You know more about power than I do. All I could do was do what I did. I was wrong at first, wanting to go. It's awkward; it's painful, even, having to refuse a president. He's been good on domestic issues. But abroad we've got to stop him from using power as if it were his rather than ours. It'll take a lot of democracy to stop that."

Ted's voice now: more questions. His respect for Cal is obviously considerable; his courtesy is total. It occurs to me that Kennedy Boston is astounded to find patrician Boston so passionately informed.

". . . I'm conscience bound." Cal stops, then starts again: "We're not only corrupting them, we're corrupting ourselves in the process."

I catch this just coming back into the Shed. The fire has burned low, but none of us seems to have wanted to turn on any lights. In the heavy dusk, the voice at the center of the room is, hauntingly, the voice of an assassinated president.

Ted stops. Then everything quiets.

Cal has had his say.

They came late, and have stayed long. It is only mid-August; but now that everybody is leaving and saying thanks, we are each noticing and saying all at once the same thing: how quickly the dark has come down.[24]

Ted Kennedy remained in touch with Booth, especially through the late 1970s. They corresponded on a number of occasions, particularly when Kennedy was asked, in May 1977, to speak at the dedication of Robert Frost's Derry, New Hampshire, farmhouse as an historic site. (Frost had died, at the age of eighty-eight, in 1963.) Kennedy sent a draft of his preliminary remarks to Booth, asking for help in enriching the text.

United States Senate
WASHINGTON, D.C. 20510

July 13, 1977

Mr. Philip Booth
Box 303
Castine, Maine 04421

Dear Philip:

I just wanted to thank you for your generous help with the draft of my remarks for the dedication of Robert Frost's home last Thursday.

Although I loved and admired Robert Frost as much as you did, somehow it takes the gift of a poet to put into words such deepfelt affection and appreciation.

Your words touched the hearts of all who attended the ceremony -- and most particularly, mine.

With my warm gratitude,

Sincerely,

Ted Kennedy

Above: Letter from Ted Kennedy to Booth.

Left: 1977 arrival of Ted Kennedy when he spoke at the dedication of Frost's Derry farmhouse.

Two years later, as Kennedy prepared to run for President, he responded to Philip's letter of support in this way:

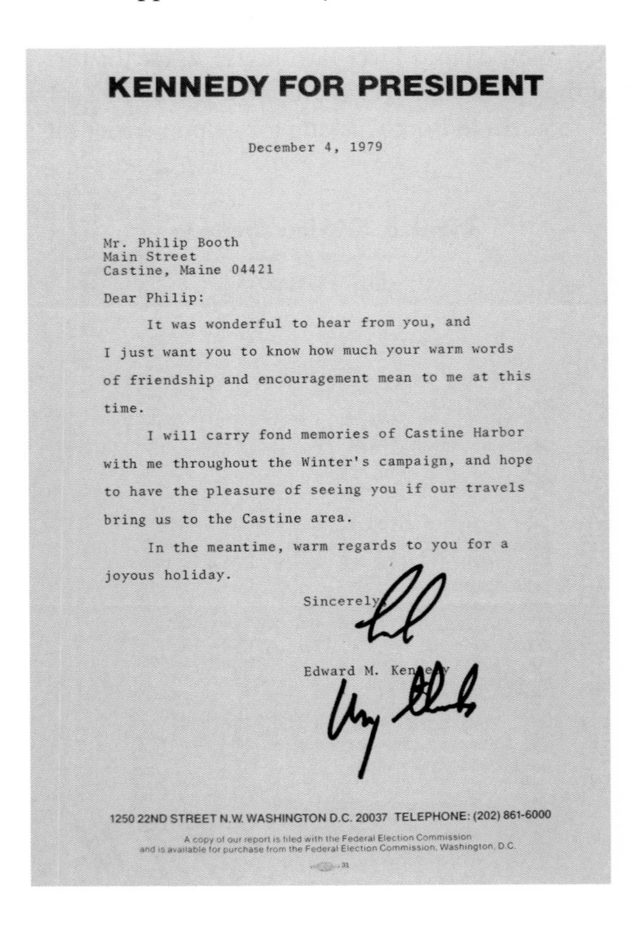

KENNEDY FOR PRESIDENT

December 4, 1979

Mr. Philip Booth
Main Street
Castine, Maine 04421

Dear Philip:

It was wonderful to hear from you, and I just want you to know how much your warm words of friendship and encouragement mean to me at this time.

I will carry fond memories of Castine Harbor with me throughout the Winter's campaign, and hope to have the pleasure of seeing you if our travels bring us to the Castine area.

In the meantime, warm regards to you for a joyous holiday.

Sincerely,

Edward M. Kennedy

1250 22ND STREET N.W. WASHINGTON D.C. 20037 TELEPHONE: (202) 861-6000

A copy of our report is filed with the Federal Election Commission and is available for purchase from the Federal Election Commission, Washington, D.C.

It was nationally and personally, however, a perilous time, one that students of my generation named the Age of Awful Assassinations. Death and loss hung heavy in the air, enshrouding not only those in public life but the world of poets.

Not only did Booth feel the loss of his mentor, Robert Frost; poets of *his* generation were also dying prematurely in the 1960s and '70s, in some instances taking their own lives. Sylvia Plath, perhaps the most famous suicide, died in the same year as Robert Frost, 1963; Randall Jarrell, after suffering two severe depressive episodes, walked in front of an oncoming car in 1965; John Berryman jumped to his death from the Washington Avenue Bridge in Minneapolis in 1972; and Anne Sexton, after having her usual companionable lunch with her closest friend, Maxine Kumin, went home, arranged herself in the car in her enclosed garage, and turned on the engine. Her death in 1974 seemed to confirm the cumulative perils of being a poet during these turbulent decades in American history; Booth, who enjoyed a close friendship with Maxine Kumin, wrote a note upon learning of Sexton's death. Kumin's response not only describes what, for her, was a devastating tragedy, but also predicts the rush of books about enormously talented and enormously self-destructive contemporary American poets.

MAXINE KUMIN
40 BRADFORD ROAD
NEWTON HIGHLANDS, MASS. 02161

27 October, 1974

Dear Philip,

Thank you for writing and for caring. Anne suffered so much and fought so hard against her demons and stayed alive so much longer than any of us had a right to expect, that I cannot help but accept her suicide for what I feel she intended this time -- not a stage play, but the final sleep she could keep, the one she so desperately wanted.

Yes, we were best friends to the end, though the closeness of the bond is something I cannot really write about. I don't think she wanted to be the center of a necrophiliac cult. But, of course, it will happen.

Enjoy your leave. Stay well, stay alive.

with love,

Maxine

Robert Lowell stopped coming to Castine in the early 1970s, partly the consequence of increasing health problems (the return of manic episodes and worsening heart problems, which would eventually be diagnosed as congestive heart failure), and partly because of a new love interest. After twenty-three years of marriage to Elizabeth Hardwick, in 1970 he left her for Caroline Blackwood, a titled Irish beauty and an heir to the Guinness fortune. They married in 1971, had a child, but the marriage failed. When Harvard offered him a teaching post, he returned from Ireland, dividing his time between Cambridge and New York, where he renewed his connections with Lizzie and Harriet. In June of 1977, Lizzie confided to Mary McCarthy that there was "no great renewed romance, but a kind of friendship and listening to his grief." Lowell, Lizzie, and Harriet returned to Castine that summer. Cousin Harriet's old house on School Street was gone, a casualty of the divorce, but Lizzie had renovated the Barn to make it quite livable and cozy.

Elizabeth Hardwick and Robert Lowell
in Castine, August 1977.

Poets on the beach, August 1977:
Richard Eberhart, Booth, Daniel Hoffman, Robert Lowell."

In August, Philip Booth decided to organize what he called "a poets' reunion," summoning colleagues who shared years of friendship and who also owned summer homes in the Penobscot Bay area. Richard Eberhart, the dean of the group and Lowell's first mentor, had a summer home, Overcliff, in Cape Rosier; Daniel Hoffman, the poet and critic who enjoyed a long career teaching at the University of Pennsylvania, also summered in Cape Rosier; Booth and Lowell came over from nearby Castine ("twenty-six miles by car, six by boat"). Eberhart's home provided an expanse of beach on which the poets walked and talked; Cal Lowell, in the last month of his life, enjoyed the good talk and high spirits, and especially his cigarettes and drink, ignoring the advice of his doctors. Striding along the rocky beach, the quartet stopped for a moment, striking a memorable tableau—one luckily caught on camera by Hoffman's wife, Elizabeth McFarland.

In September, Lowell made a final trip to Ireland to explain to Blackwood that he had decided to return to the States permanently. The trip, not surprisingly, was a disaster, and on September 12 he quickly boarded a plane back home, landing in New York. He hailed a cab to Hardwick's New York apartment on West 67th Street. Upon arrival, the cabdriver found him slumped over in the backseat, dead of a heart attack. Philip's telegram to Lizzie spoke of the enormity of her and his loss and acknowledged that perhaps Cal, who had said, tellingly, years earlier,

Ms. Eli-abeth Hardwick
15 West 67th Street
NYC 10023 212-724-1468

At least this last summer.
Ulysses' exhaustion perhaps after all the light
of the world. Surely the poems his strip of
eternity.

Our love to you and to Harriet.

"Everybody's tired of my turmoil," was finally at peace.

Although Lowell was gone, his impact on Booth was enduring. Booth would long remember what he would call "one of the most generous things I know"—that summer afternoon in the barn when Lowell had "risked" an honest and searching criticism of Booth's early poems. Booth had been heard by one of the finest poets of his generation; thereafter he determined to sail "in deeper water."

October 12th
1955

Dear Cal,

For a month now I have been thinking toward what thanks could be adequate for your comment on my poems, and for a month I have known that no thanks was sufficient to such generous talk. I've held off saying even that, hoping; wanting to find good words pared down to truth: the hard clarity of the Northwest wind, the splintered sunlight on the harbor, the beach that is rock, and shingle-nails sticking into my back where I leaned against Miss Winslow's shipwreck barn and felt your insight work.

It should be a poem, but it is not; half because I have been reading instead of writing, half because I had to take all sorts of new bearings after weathering out the squalls of your criticism, squalls that did not knock me down but only keep driving me ahead under shortened sail. I suppose I want most of all to thank you for risking so much; it is one of the most generous things I know. Whether I'll write better is with time and the gods, but I'd like to think that I already know how to teach better for being so well taught.

Wellesley seems now to take all my time, and all my overtime thought. Freshmen conferences, ideas for papers, talktalktalk and correcting: you know these too. Somehow it is worth it (quite beyond all cliches about a teacher's rewards), but when the first-ofthe-year push is on it can also mean the frustration that means no poems. Maybe B.U. is different, but I doubt it.

Sometime soon, in whatever lull there is, Margaret and I want very much to get you both out here for a meal. Or come whenever you're this way, feeling some country need, for tea or potluck. Perhaps I should report in advance that --without you as crew -- we managed to put Ariel on a Horseshoe Creek rock when we tacked her back in a near gale. We'd almost made the mooring when we hit, and we were only saved redder faces than we had (mostly mine) when Vaughn the boatbuilder admitted that our particular rock wasn't on any chart. No damage to the hull, pride turned to humility, and a great deal learned in getting off toward deeper water. I mean that about the poems, too, and more thanks than it is easy to say.

One of the last photos of Robert Lowell, gone within a month.

Heading Out

By the mid-'80s, Castine had become the primary residence for Philip and Margaret Booth; although Booth continued to teach for several more years at Syracuse, clustering his courses into one semester, Castine, its population of native Castiners mixed with "the summer people" who came to their homes and cottages from the Fourth of July to Labor Day, became his year-round community. Old friends and fellow poets increasingly came to Castine for visits: Richard Eberhart and Daniel Hoffman had summer homes nearby, as did Fred Morgan, editor of the *Hudson Review*. Maxine Kumin and her husband, Victor, came in the mid-'80s; Stephen Dunn and Wesley McNair visited a few years later. Bob and Carol Allen by then had their own home in Castine, as did Peter Davis and his wife. Booth's boyhood friend from Hanover days, David Bradley, had for years summered in nearby Brooklin and visited often; old family friends Andrews Wanning and his wife, Patricia, sailed over from their place in Blue Hill, and E. B. White's son, Joel, ran a boatyard in Brooklin that serviced a number of the sailboats Booth's friends used. If the chances of seeing Philip Booth were greatly increased if you went to Castine rather than expecting him to come to you, the continuous migration also reflected the popularity of Castine as a summer home destination, a magnet for those who enjoyed recreational boating and fishing—yoked to a thriving arts community.

Robin Booth, the youngest daughter of the Booths and hence the last to leave home, pondered her father's ongoing exploration of where he belonged and how Castine played into the process:

> *I think Dad sometimes experienced a split in his loyalties in Castine—and it left him, at times, not knowing quite where he*

belonged. There were native Castiners, hardworking men and women, many of whom he grew up with. He admired their strength and resilience and loved their friendliness and humor. On the other hand, Castine, at least in the summers, was home to many writers and artists, and he was counted among them. I don't know that he ever felt asked to choose one over the other, but there were two distinct communities, something I came to understand more clearly when I took high school summer jobs waitressing or working at the Castine drugstore. Dad must have, at times, felt himself caught somewhere in between them."[1]

Robin Booth with her father, August 1985.

Years later one of Booth's granddaughters, Caroline Pinkston, examined some of the same questions as she recalled experiences she had as a child with her grandfather and insights she later gleaned from his poems:

> *Like many Maine towns, Castine's rhythms are dictated by the seasons: in the summer the town's population almost doubles with an influx of what the locals call "summer people." And like many Maine towns, the relationship between the summer people and the locals is complicated. Castine is a small, close-knit place and most locals would tell you that the summer people are nice enough, but they don't really get Castine, or even really try to. In a poem called "The Incredible Yachts," my grandfather once said of some of the summer people that they didn't care "to know in truth / what harbor they were in. / "*
>
> *For my grandfather, "knowing the harbor you're in" was*

> *a guiding principle, and he lived out that principle in Castine. He knew every corner of Castine and just about everyone in it—he was friends with both the literary circle and the guys who worked at the dock. He gave sailing lessons to local kids and had practically memorized the coastline. He was beloved in Castine because he loved the town so deeply, and it was the beating heart of his poetry. But I'm also learning that while you have to know your harbor, you also have to step beyond it. That's the riddle my grandfather grappled with, one that I think is worth examining.*[2]

Down the coast in Rockland, Maine, photographer Peter Ralston and ecologist and writer Philip Conkling were trying their own experiment in "knowing the harbor you're in." They joined forces to establish the Island Institute, a nonprofit organization formed in the mid-'80s to assist islanders in sustaining their communities in the Gulf of Maine and keeping their islands economically, socially, and ecologically sound. The institute and its beautifully produced annual magazine, *Island Journal,* had a significant impact on Philip Booth in the last two decades of his writing life. He was deeply sensitive to and supportive of their mission, and they were delighted to have a poet of his accomplishments offer poems, an article on photography, and a lengthy interview to the *Journal*.

Ralston and Conkling wanted the Maine islands to remain self-sustaining working communities, not simply picturesque backdrops for tourist postcards or summer escapes for the wealthy; they knew many were struggling and some were on the brink of being abandoned. Conkling brought to this new mission a training in forestry and ecology, and the experience of a life-changing summer on Hurricane Island, home to a sea-based school of Outward Bound, which hired him to write a guide to the natural history of the islands. Ralston, a self-taught freelance photographer, deepened his craft through a close friendship with painter Andrew Wyeth and his wife, Betsy. Chadds Ford, Pennsylvania, neighbors of Ralston's family, they became in his words, "second parents, higher educators, mentors." When the Wyeths summered in Maine, then moved there permanently, Ralston went along, photographing Wyeth's paintings for professional marketing;

subsequently, he voyaged out to photograph Southern Island and Allen Island, the latter acquired by Betsy Wyeth in the hope that it could serve a local community of fishermen and also sustain a summer community. The Island Institute was the nonprofit organization designed by Wyeth, Ralston, and Conkling to fund, enrich and sustain island communities; the *Journal*, with a wide mix of articles appealing to both the scientific and the arts-minded, was its beautiful avatar, with full-page breathtaking color photographs by Ralston and a mix of multidisciplinary articles and poems designed to "celebrate Maine's island communities."

In the fall of 1986, Conkling went to Castine to meet and talk with Philip Booth; Ralston followed in the winter of '87, taking a series of evocative photographs of Booth. The interview and images were published in the 1988 annual edition of the *Journal*. Conkling recalls:

> *I can remember almost exactly to the day when I met Philip Booth. I had read his poetry for years—which I first discovered sometime in the late '70s after I had spent long stints on Hurricane Island and then wintering over on Vinalhaven. His poems "The Islanders" and "Matinicus" went right through me like a clearing wind. I felt—like many of his readers—that he had written something for me personally.*
>
> *I was the unofficial poetry editor of Island Journal, and in volume 3 we ran those two poems of Philip Booth's with permission from his publisher (and him). Then in the fall of 1987, I called him up in Castine and asked to interview him for the 1988 fifth issue of the Journal, to which he graciously assented. I spent most of the afternoon with him in Castine on that November day, first in his kitchen and then later in his living room. It didn't take much time for me to detect the poet at work in the interview: his intense scrutiny of the landscape, his curiosity about the community and its interrelationships, his precise use of language (you could almost feel him wince when he heard a word inaccurately used)—all of these things figure in his poems. I was the acolyte and he the mentor in this conversation; at the same time he was generous with his time and open with me, even when revealing some darker moments*

in his past: his grandfather's depression and his mother's illness.

His replies to my questions about the role of the poet and his detailed response describing the influence of Robert Frost on his own poetic process were, as we say on the water, "full and by." He also said something that spoke directly to my heart: "The amazing thing about poems, like the amazing thing about islands: to those people to whom they matter, they matter a very great deal. That they exist, that they are there."

I remember asking him if he would submit a poem to the Journal that might accompany the interview, and he shot back, quickly, "I don't write on demand." But of course he thought about it and somewhat later submitted "Wanting," a poem that had just been published in Ploughshares. I think it is one of his finest in his later years: the voice is clear, strong, and bleakly honest—and that is the voice I heard that afternoon in Castine.[3]

Discovering where one belongs, a recurrent theme in Booth's poems, became a central focus in the poems he wrote in the final years of his artistic productivity. The process of discovery, initially, involves risk and how one responds to it. His metaphors of sailing beyond chart and compass, or walking to the edge and contemplating stepping off or stepping back, are vehicles for examining the value of knowing oneself and confronting one's fears. Yet this was a process that began very early in Booth's life, as described by his godson, Ben Bradley, the son of Booth's great friend David Bradley.

David Bradley, after graduating from Dartmouth in 1938 and attending Harvard Medical School, became a surgeon and antinuclear advocate, whose best-selling book *No Place to Hide* offered an account of postwar atomic tests on Bikini Atoll in the South Pacific, warning about the dangers of radiation fallout. Bradley was also a first-rate skier and ski jumper, good enough to earn an invitation to the 1940 Olympics, later canceled by the outbreak of the war. A decade older, he came to know the young Booth in Hanover because of their mutual love of skiing and ski jumping.

As Ben Bradley recalls, "In later years Philip and Margaret were my parents' closest friends. But my father used to tell stories about how he got to know Philip in the early Hanover days; he remembered one winter day in particular when Philip, though still in high school, managed to set the record on the Middlebury ski jump. Dad said that the two jumpers before Philip made his attempt had crashed. And in those days that meant that rescue guys on a toboggan (they called it the meat wagon) came out to pick up the fallen jumper. Here was Philip as a high schooler, jumping against college jumpers, watching the first two crash. The whole point of a successful jump is to hit the takeoff exactly right. It requires a very good athlete with absolute focus, and one who is pretty fearless. And Philip executed it perfectly, setting the hill record."[4]

In a revealing article he published in the *Christian Science Monitor* in 1987, Booth recounted this experience and likened the courage and thrill of ski jumping to "a poem as distilled, formal, and symbolically liberating as a haiku."[5] Describing the process of "leaning all the way out," as he titled the article, he used the particulars of a successful jump to evoke the feelings a successful poem produces:

> *Northern hills. A ski jump looming over the snowy backside of a gray northern town. On top of the jump, cold, level with the treetops, a kid, waiting for the wind to calm. He sights the glazed track down to its end: the valley there is no bottom of. The valley where—if he has not fallen—he'll slow, and turn, to what he may dream is the crowd's Olympic applause.*
>
> *For the jumper, like the pilot of a jet, takeoff and landing are crucial. For the ski jumper, who is not only his own pilot but his own plane, and whose flight lands almost as soon as it begins, everything depends on takeoff. So, too, for a diver or pole-vaulter, whose events are comparably instantaneous. But vaulter and diver start comparatively slowly and, unlike the jumper, can see where they're going to land or splash down. The jumper cannot, as he starts down the steeply concave in-run, see much beyond the takeoff; nor can he see over the knoll to the landing as he approaches the takeoff at some 60 m.p.h.*
>
> *At such speed, the takeoff is all. Once he tips his long*

David Bradley and Booth sailing in Castine in 1992.

skis down into the in-run chute, the jumper is irretrievably committed. That he could possibly fall on the in-run must not occur to him. He crouches to cut the wind resistance in the brief seconds he has to gain velocity for his flight, his eyes fixed on the lip of the takeoff. Beyond that lip is, literally, nothing. He must concentrate every sense to compute the exact instant when he should start his leap, which is itself being completed as his ski-tips reach the lip of what is, suddenly, an abyss. At precisely the right instant he has, by then, with all the power his legs can release, sprung up to gain altitude over the knoll, and begun to dive forward to form his body into an airfoil parallel to the skis now planing under him.

Strength matters, but coordination and timing matter more. Courage is a given. Yet compared to downhill racing, ski jumping is not as dangerous as it looks. Unless the jumper leaps before the takeoff helps catapult him, and air pressure thus catches his tips so that they tend to trip him into a somersault, most falls are simply bad tumbles down the steep landing. The bigger the hill, the more powerful the forces: On jumps designed for 65 meters or more, the duration and height of a jumper's soaring involve him in such subtle control as using his hands as ailerons. Even there, as on smaller jumps, where there is less pressure under his chest and skis, how he handles his takeoff is a controlling factor.

Aside from such uncontrollable factors as sudden turbulence, or the terrifying arrival of a stray dog on the outrun, the jumper who rides the air with a quietness balanced by courage is, in effect, home free. On even a small-scale hill, his being airborne gives him what is, both literally and metaphorically, a natural high.

High and free. Not wide. Jumping is not the Whitmanesque free-form flight of hang gliding, but a poem as distilled, formal, and symbolically liberating as a haiku. A jumper's freedom owes to the form his takeoff allows in the air. For an instant, given the speed to which gravity brought him on the in-run, he seems suddenly free of gravity. Gravity will, of course, haul him home near the red line on the landing that warns him not to out-jump the hill. But in the air, if he has released himself into it with due control, a jumper is demonstrably and privately free.

The kid waiting at the top of the in-run knows. Or soon will. He's one of thousands of kids all over Scandinavia and Northern Europe, all over the Soviet Union, Japan, Canada, and America crouching for the speed, feeling the air lift them, tumbling down landings, or hearing another kid yell a good word when they turn at the end of the out-run. He's one of the kids out practicing this February afternoon in Brattleboro, Lebanon, Ishpeming, and Duluth, kids who'll in a few years be jumping in the traditional Washington's Birthday events on such big hills as Lake Placid, Steamboat Springs, and Iron Mountain.

I was one of those kids, hopping off bumps when I was 8,

> *building small snow jumps in the back pasture when I was 10, testing myself on a 20-meter at 12, a 40-meter at 15. Rites of passage, all. I've seen photographs of my jumping that clearly remind me of what a mediocre jumper I mostly was. I often flailed the air and, as my courage wobbled, fell. Once, after two previous jumpers had fallen, I steeled myself not to, and held the Middlebury hill record for five minutes, until a first-rate jumper leaped farther with a grace I usually lacked. I was average, at best. I was often scared, not on natural in-runs, but on high trestles I could barely make myself climb.*
>
> *I have nightmares about those trestles still. But when I have lain awake with larger fears, or have been painfully aware of my body's limits, I have also known in some innermost part of myself that—among hundreds and hundreds of times on an in-run—I did, perhaps five or eight times, hit the takeoff so perfectly that I did not pull back but leaned all the way out on my luck, and once was so still in the air that I not only saw the crowd, and a girl in the crowd, but sailed somehow out of myself and, for an eternal instant, jumping, could see myself jumping, and knew I saw myself clear.*

"Sailing out of myself" in order to "see myself clear" is, for Booth, an initial step in discovering "where one belongs." If the early poems are arresting in their imagining of existence at the edge of things, an edge the narrator deliberately carves and studies as surely as the ski jumper intently focuses on the "lip of the takeoff," the later poems explore more fully the pull of belonging—to family, to history, to nature, to community. Edges will always appear in Booth's poems, but an edge comes to define not only the solitary seeker but, reflexively, where the narrator "came from" and what he can learn about his life before that edge is erased: before the tide leaves the shoreline, or the light fails, or sleep overtakes him. The magnetic pull of the community, where he is "relative to every last house," is a force as compelling and as revelatory as "sailing out of myself."

Before Sleep

The day put away before bed,
the house almost closed before night.

By the time I walk out over the knoll,
down the steep Main Street

that dead-ends in the sea,
the village has put out its lights.

The winter stars are turned up over
the tide, a tide so quiet the harbor

holds stars. The planet holds.
Before the village turns over in sleep,

I stand at the edge of the tide,
letting my feet feel into the hillside

to where my dead ancestors live.
Whatever I know before sleep

surrounds me. I cannot help know.
By blood or illness, gossip or hope,

I'm relative to every last house.
Before I climb home up the hill, I hold:

I wait for myself to quiet, breathing
the breath of sleepers I cannot help love.

If Booth's early fascinations were with Frost's conflicted narrator, viewing two paths diverging in a wood, or Melville's "isolatoes" who, like Father Mapple, deliver their sermons from elevated pulpits and then pull up the ladder of access, increasingly his later poems explore the "affinities," commonalities, "relations" among people, their situations, their hopes and dreams, their successes and failures.

The writers to whom Booth returned again and again for sustenance and insight—the Melville of Ishmael and Queequeg, the quiet but devastatingly discerning Chekhov, and especially Eudora Welty, with her habit of presenting, through her home community in Jackson, Mississippi, a whole universe of thought and feeling drawn exactly to scale—explored the values of belonging to community. Booth's interest in capturing some sense of a unified human experience and rendering it in more lyrical ways lies at the heart of many of his later poems; it may also reflect his promise to himself and to the memory of Cal Lowell to "sail in deeper waters."

~

In a letter to Sue Ely dated Labor Day 1986, Booth wrote of finalizing the paperwork associated with his retirement at Syracuse:

> *It's a great relief to me to have decided all this, and to have it, after some three months of negotiations, stamped in gold and all but sealed, by various chairs and deans. Retirement from teaching means that I'd be able to write the better and the more. But it also means, God willing, more sailing than I/we were able to achieve this summer, and more woodlot work, and more walking the shore to listen to how it all feels.*

Listening "to how it all feels" and developing the techniques to record those feelings in freer ways became more evident in the poems of the next dozen years when Booth published *Relations: Selected Poems 1950–1985* (1986), *Selves* (1990), *Pairs* (1994), and *Lifelines: Selected Poems 1950–1999* (1999), which received the 2001 Poets' Prize. How to relinquish such tight control of the poetic line was on his mind when he was interviewed in Castine by Philip Conkling in 1987. In that conversation Booth was exploring what subtle—even subliminal—influences Frost had had on his poems and on other poets of his generation.

Booth with his great friend and dedicated correspondent, Sue Ely, in Castine in 1987.

> *I've tried to sort out in my mind what I learned from him. I think Richard Wilbur said, while being interviewed about some poems, that Mr. Frost in effect let poems "come in on him" rather than going out to them through complex formal structures. I hadn't thought of that being a Frostian thing particularly. But I think Dick is right that Mr. Frost allowed himself poems. . . . Obviously I have moved from writing rather formal, highly structured poems, early, to opening myself to much different kinds of poems as I've gone on.*[6]

He adds, in observations published as "Selected Fragments" less than a year later: "You must let the poems speak to you; you must let the poem tell you how it wants to be. . . . All writing is a closing off and an opening; even within a poem these pressures and relaxations show themselves in how the poem moves, how it paces itself."[7]

This "opening out" process, letting the poem in, was aided by Booth's love of music and especially jazz, his love of the language patterns of native Mainers, and his increasing fascination with photography.

The influence of jazz, especially its use of syncopated rhythms, appeared in some earlier poems that use enjambed lines to spill meaning into longer units of thought or feeling. Booth was also fond of using the "offbeat" in poetic lines, which he termed "analogous to a drummer adding a hi-hat to the snare and bass he's already working." As he told Stephen Dunn:

> *When I was a kid, about thirteen or fourteen, partially growing up here [Castine] and partially in Hanover, I used to sneak into the Dartmouth College spring houseparty dances. I'd sneak into the top floor of the gym at four in the afternoon and hide under the bandstand until I got kicked out about nine-thirty at night. I listened close-in to Jimmy Dorsey, Jimmy Lunceford, Louis Armstrong, a lot of them. They had two bands playing opposite sets, as they did in the big dance halls in Harlem. One wonderful time after I got kicked out and went downstairs, there was a fine musician named Sy Oliver who was down there picking out on the piano, writing, actually writing what has always been one of my favorite songs as a metaphor for what we're talking about: "T'ain't what you do, it's the way what you do it. Ain't what you say, it's the way what you say it." I totally remember hearing him hum that, pick out the notes, and say it. I don't know nearly as much about jazz as some poets do . . . but I feel very strongly about the way rhythms inhere in certain kinds of language.*[8]

To listen to one's own interior voice and "the way rhythms inhere in certain kinds of language" is the given of any good poet. As Mary Oliver writes in her book *Winter Hours*: "In the act of writing the poem, I am obedient and submissive. Insofar as one can, I put aside ego and vanity, and even intention. I listen. What I hear is almost a voice, almost a language. It is a second ocean, rising, singing into one's ear, or deep inside the ears, whispering in the recesses where one is less oneself than a part of some single indivisible community."

Stephen Dunn visits Booth in Castine in the fall of 1991. Posing in front of several cords of firewood, Booth quips that "these two poets are more accustomed to splitting infinitives than wood these days."

Whether music is defined as that oceanic language Mary Oliver hears or the ways rhythms inhere in the music Booth loved all his life, his poems reveal a variety of experiments with aural effects—particularly how speech and breath beats and cadence shape meaning.

Down East speech, with its peculiar stress on syllables within a word, its understatement, its short, clipped phrases, offers its own version of syncopation. Booth, after many years of listening to and collecting stories told by native Castiners, became a skilled storyteller. Cal Lowell, in particular, but also other guests at dinner parties or on sailing excursions, would beg him to tell certain stories in "his Maine voice." He begins his elegy to Lowell in that voice.

This Day After Yesterday

Robert Traill Spence Lowell (1917–1977)

I
This day after yesterday.

Morning rain small on the harbor,
nothing that's not gray.

I heard at Hooper's, taking the Plymouth in
for brakes. Out from behind
his rolltop desk, Ken said, "*Ra*dio says
a *col*league of yours died. Yessir,
*died. Low*ell. Wasn't he your friend?"

Though the poem, prompted by Lowell's death, is layered with grief and truth-telling, soaring to incorporate images from Ulysses's journey and return, it starts in a very different register, in the voices of Castine villagers making their inquiries about that "*col*league of yours." The line stops and starts, an irregular heartbeat.

Sailing, with its rhythmic shifts, also influenced the shape and rhythm of Booth's poems, as he suggested in his interview with Stephen Dunn after the publication of *Relations*. In searching for language that would also "allow the poem in," he drew this analogy: "I think there is a resistance [in the use of words] that is more like the resistance of sailing to windward and having to tack by necessity as the wind changes slightly. There is a kind of prosody . . . which allows one to sail with beautiful freedoms within a closed course."[9]

When asked by Dunn whether he felt he wrote in a distinctive voice, he replied: "I don't think about 'voice' as such; I talk aloud to myself when I write, but I mostly listen for rhythms and how they get shaped and paced by internal patterns of sound. I suppose I have a New England voice, in some large sense, direct, slightly flat, perhaps dry . . . a kind of understatement that's not (however wry) without some sense of humor."[10]

Despite the aural techniques Booth employed in a number of his poems, readers of his poetry, both admirers and detractors, have commented less on his "voice" than on the instantly recognizable visual structure of many of his poems, particularly those written early in his career: short lines arranged as a column on the page, surrounded by white space, cut by sharp margins, terse to the point of implosion. Those who admired the effect suggested that his method was the embodiment of stripping away the inessential: getting to the essence of things. Detractors suggested that too much was left out for real access to the meaning; the poem became a tower in which the poet had barricaded himself. Despite evidence to the contrary—a loosening of the poetic line, increased use of aural effects rendering sound at least as important as the "look" of a poem—reviewers frequently returned to the "tower poems" as the prototypes of Booth's art.

When the poet Wesley McNair traveled to Castine in December 1991 after a poetry reading of his own in nearby Blue Hill, he spent the evening and following day with the Booths. Gathering his recollections into a major essay on Booth's unchanging, and then changing, prosody published in *Mapping the Heart: Reflections on Place and Poetry,* he reassessed the overall effect of the "word tower" poems. He argues that, because of their compression, their short lines, their implied but never fully delineated feelings, Booth risks "leaving too much out."

"One cannot avoid the theme of containment for long, or resist seeing the poem as a kind of container or compartment—a booth," he says. "[T]he booth of a Booth poem is . . . an enclosure, its arrangement of words, phrases and stanzas a puzzle of the deconstructed sentence that we must, by applying mind and feeling, put together."[11] But as he reflects further, he alights on the poem "Presence," one collected in *Selves*, which he calls "my own favorite in that book," and which departs radically from the tight control of earlier poems.

Following a reading of his poems in nearby Blue Hill,
Wesley McNair visits with Booth in December 1991;
snow has already begun in Castine.

McNair observes, "Putting short lines aside, he uses long ones for 'Presence'; whereas his less characteristic long-lined poems are continuously enjambed, this verse combines enjambment with end-stopping, giving the line an unusual freedom as it shapes the poem's long sentences. The result is a Whitmanesque inclusiveness that is wholly remarkable. Booth unboothed."[12]

Presence

after George Oppen

That we are here: that we can question who
we are, where; that we relate to how deer

once small have grown bold in our back garden;
that we can ask, ask even ourselves, how

to the other we may appear, here in the always near place
we seem to ourselves to inhabit, who sleep toward

and wake from steeped hills, the sea opening into our eyes
the infinite possibility of infinity

we believe we're neither beyond nor shy of,
here as we are, without doubt, amid then, there,

and now, falling through dark into light, and back,
against which we cannot defend, wish as we might, as we do.

Still, as the physicist said, *the mystery is*
that we are here, here at all, still bearing with,

and borne by, all we try to make sense of:
this evening two does and a fawn who browse

the head lettuce we once thought was ours.
But no. As we chase them off mildly, and make

an odd salad of what they left us, the old stars
come casually out, and we see near and far we own nothing:

it's us who belong to all else; who, given this day,
are touched by, and touch, our tenderest knowing,

our lives incalculably dear as we feel for each other,
our skin no more or less thin than that of redwing,

rainbow, star-nose, or whitethroat, enfolded like us
in the valleys and waves of this irrefutable planet.

McNair emphasizes not only the longer, more undulating aural effects in the poem, but also the inclusiveness of its themes: here, at land's end, Booth balances a sense of individual self with the recognition of connection, the natural community to which all living things belong. And, in fact, the opening-out process McNair celebrates in this poem recurs in several of Booth's most memorable later poems, including "Coming To," "Again, the Solstice," and "Passage without Rites."

But it would be too easy, reductive even, to suggest that all or even the majority of Booth's poems in his last two writing decades abandon the taut, compressed forms his early work displayed, or the stark honesty of the poet's gaze. He simply found other ways of capturing the connections to a larger community of living beings. Take, for example, "Wanting," the poem Philip Conkling nominated as "one of the finest poems of Booth's later years."

Wanting

Coastal rain, an iron sky.
Granite mainland, granite island.
It's too cold, I'm too cold,

to row across to the mainland.
The pickup needs an inspection;
I ought to row over across and

drive her to Gray for a sticker.
Let it wait. There's still time.
There's time this morning to

read the whole day, to read
the cold rain, the old sky, the who-
do-I-think-I-am. Between five

and seven, the crown of the day
no matter what weather, who can afford
less wonder. Or bear any more?

I'm in the kitchen, belonging
with what doesn't know me, so far
as I know; pots and pans that

heat up and cool, belonging by how
I feel about them, not how they
maybe feel about me. Beings who

differently breathe, we humans
contract—in and out—to expand
all our lives. Who in hell would I be

if I couldn't imagine, imagine
the range of this moment in
the spun flight, the spun life

of the planet? It's here, when
anyone pays due attention:
here now, there then in the now

where anyone opens to feel it.
Now, shaving, I long to pay back
what I owe, however much, in

the mirror. I find myself
wanting. Wanting in all
directions, across distance

measured in minutes as well
as degrees. Now, outdoors,
out under ospreys wheeling over

a tidestream, searching the shallows
for alewives, I look up with
my own hunger. Hunger, how

can I mean it, given
lives starving? I want to mean
how-can-I-not, to have

their lives at heart, stretching
not reaching as their lives
contract, while my life

is weighed with alternatives.
How can I possibly mean,
give what to whom, given

this glassy sea I cannot
see much beyond, this island
that embraces my waking: this spruce,

deermoss, this lichen, and you
in time I want far from here
to touch, the you in far different light

who is differently focused, more
or less caring or careless, while
I move under the high pitched birds

and—by long inclination—lift
myself over the dark march of ants
crossing the bedrock granite.

Stare. Educate the eye.
Die knowing something.
You are not here long.
—Walker Evans

Let Us Now Praise Famous Men, the riveting collaboration combining the prose of James Agee with the photographs of Walker Evans, became an American classic by the 1950s. Evans, known particularly for his Depression-era photography, set out in 1936 on a *Fortune* magazine assignment with Agee to explore and record the daily lives of tenant farmers in the Deep South. Their account, which became one of the most widely read books of the twentieth century, offered a portrait of place, of the people who worked and shaped the land, the homes they occupied, the children they raised, the conditions under which they worked.

The work of Walker Evans, which Booth admired greatly and mentioned on a number of occasions in his correspondence, coupled with a close friendship with New England-based photographer Rollie McKenna, intensified Booth's interest in photography.[13] Henry Miller recalls Booth years earlier as "primarily observant," and Wesley McNair has emphasized his early affinities with painters like John Marin. But by the late 1980s Booth's interest in photography moved from hobby status to creative experimentation. How does the photographer work—and from what distance? How does he or she offer access, new ways of seeing and understanding people and places? What elements of any given scene should receive primary focus, and why? These were questions Booth was asking.

By 1991, Booth was beginning to talk about his experimentation in poetic technique in terms of photography. In a short interview in "Compass," a weekend supplement to the *Castine Patriot*, March 21, 1991, Booth explains his growing interest in photography: "I think my focal length has changed over the years. Although my observation used to be from a standard 50-millimeter lens brought in pretty close, I now use, to extend the metaphor further, a variety of lenses and use them at different distances from what I'm writing about." In the early 1990s Booth accepted an interesting assignment from Peter Ralston: to write an extended essay on the work of Maine photographer Jeff Dworsky. The article, titled "Writing with Light," was accompanied by a folio of images shot by Dworsky and appeared in the 1992 issue of *Island Journal*. In it Booth describes photographic techniques before the digital changeover, before adjustments and enhancements made through Photoshopping became commonplace. He begins:

> *Photography is, literally, writing with light. Most of the photographs in this remarkable folio were written with winter light, in the bare*

season when island life is in no way trespassed on by tourists or pleasure boats. . . .

As his photographs clearly prove, Jeff Dworsky's eye is used to seeing through a viewfinder. Seeing, not merely looking. Whether he's carrying a camera or not, his eye observes, his mind fills with insight, his heart responds—here to the available light of humanity itself—with an acuity that no autofocus or exposure meter can measure. . . .

Jeff Dworsky's eye cares little for mere appearance. It cares duly for handsaw, hammer, potwarp, engine oil, starting-fluid, and boat paint. It cares passionately for human beings who know they live on one of this island world's smaller islands, islands where life's daily terms are daily visible. Notably visible in all but a few of these photographs is the window through which islanders forever look out, in whatever weather, to check the weather and, if it is visible, to see the sea. In winter's hardest weathers they can barely leave the house, much less the island. With so much beyond all control beyond them, generation after generation of islanders know that if they're to winter out, to make it over the old March hill, they must snug down in their kitchens, their general store, stay close to the woodshed, workbench, and woodstove. And, without choice, live close to each other.

Inhabiting such necessity, Jeff Dworsky's camera eye focuses most acutely on the basics of island life: work, love, joy, anguish, prayer, and play; on how such basics are equally shared, whether in ways lonely or communal, by women, men, children, of age after age after age. His photographs show, tellingly, how faces feel. And how, in every aspect of island experience, hands work and express. How, in extreme human weathers, hands cover faces.

Jeff Dworsky has, in an island context, made interior photographs that tell, as quietly as a Chekhov story might, how we humans survive in our most interior selves. To refamiliarize ourselves with the islanders of these photographs is to review isolated aspects of our own lives, to find anew the essential community to which we inescapably belong.

Even as he focuses on the evocative images of Jeff Dworsky, Booth may be describing—consciously or unconsciously—his own evolving artistic process. The frame through which the photographer looks approximates Booth's own outlook/insight metaphors. Dworsky's images of the particulars of islanders' daily existence—the tools, woodsheds, woodstoves, workbenches essential to their survival—are avenues into their "interior life," a technique Booth employed as early as "Eaton's Boatyard." Most tellingly, what Booth especially honors in Dworsky's work is his capacity to respond "to the available light of humanity itself." Booth observed elsewhere, "The world's not apt to be resolved by a poem"—[or a photograph, for that matter]—"but a poem can make the world's landscape more humanly bearable, maybe more bearably human."[14]

~

If retirement brought the rewards of uninterrupted writing time and year-round residence in Castine, the old balancing act continued. In a letter to Susan Ely dated September 15, 1988, Booth was already worrying about the considerable upkeep to the Castine home. Some portion of the large white clapboard structure required repainting every summer, and the repairs and renovations required for any 150-year-old structure occurred with discouraging frequency. As he observed to Ely, "[This] house is a large matter in itself, a constant concern of economics and indecision. But no matter all the logic of what closes in around us in fact, and locally; the counter is that it's late in our lives to break the chain of the family who've lived here. Could I/we leave my/our own attachments here? Could we even go beyond the very village were we to leave? Who knows."

David Hatch, who grew up in Castine and later established a successful painting and drywall business in town, for many years handled the painting and renovations on the Booth house, the McCarthy house, and the Lowell house; he understood the reverence Booth had for his ancestral home and also the vexations surrounding its constant upkeep. Hatch recalls:

> *I worked on a number of the houses of the literary summer residents, and gradually became responsible for maintaining them during the winter months. But I knew Margaret and Phil the best*

of the group. Not only were they in town for much longer stretches of time, but I grew up knowing Phil. When I was about eight years old, I signed up to take sailing lessons through the Castine Yacht Club. The club was a hub for all of us who loved the water and wanted to learn to sail and watch the races it sponsored each year. Phil was commodore of the club when I signed up. After a certain amount of instruction, we went out for a sail—the kids in their boats with their instructors and Phil in his own boat, watching and helping us learn. The outing included only one overnight, but when I got back I felt like I had sailed to China.

I can hardly remember a time when I didn't know Phil and Margaret, for they were a real part of life in Castine. I even shared a year in school with Robin Booth, when she decided to stay in Castine through the winter. Phil always took a special interest in my work on the house and he left very detailed lists of repairs he needed. He knew everybody in town and walked every day, stopping to chat with passersby. He turned up regularly at town meetings too, though he rarely stood up to speak. There was nothing self-serving in his participation; he was simply interested in the life of the town he cared about so much. Almost everybody in town remembers Phil charging down the hill when a fire alarm sounded, in order to direct traffic at the Court Street intersection.

As my family and business grew he always inquired about my kids or responded thoughtfully when I asked for advice about my business. For years he remembered my kids' birthdays, writing and sending them a poem on their special day. And he gave me the best business advice I ever received, a simple sentence that I still think about every day: "You never know how another person feels; get the full story."

Phil's contributions to Castine were visible to many, but fewer people knew about Margaret's work in acquiring and preserving parcels of land whose scenic beauty and recreational opportunities might have been lost to developers.

Margaret Booth was a member of the fledging Castine Conservation Trust, founded in 1978 and designed to preserve and steward land for future generations to enjoy. For years Ram Island had been a popular destination for the people of Castine, Penobscot, and Brooksville, who rowed or sailed to the island to swim, fish, or camp overnight. When the property was put up for sale in 1979, the Conservation Trust, fearing the area would be lost to the public, formed the Committee to Save Ram Island; Margaret was one of four committee members charged with the responsibility of raising the $30,000 required for its purchase. Their efforts resulted in the first property purchased outright by the trust. As David Hatch observes, "Over the years Margaret and her colleagues' work saved dozens of parcels in Castine and surrounding communities. I can hardly imagine what we might have lost without their efforts."[15]

As worrisome as house maintenance and declining health might be, the rewards of living in that house in Castine, of writing in the upstairs studio looking out over the Main Street rooftops and down toward the harbor, of cutting wood at Cold Knoll (the woodlot the Booths owned a mile or so out of town), or walking the beautiful stretch of Schoolhouse Beach they'd purchased years earlier, continued to sustain and inspire. Booth's delight in having easy access to the water—and to all that it provided—registers in a letter to Ely written just two months after he recounted his worries about the house (November 27, 1988):

> *I trucked myself down to Brooklin again and sailed from cold to warm in the absolute lightest of Northerlies, tacking off the mooring and out of Center Harbor, and across the Reach, and all the way up to the Benjamin River entrance/mouth, which makes a fine little harbor at Sedgwick. All the way being maybe three miles by osprey, but maybe twice that what with tacking in air so light I could hear seals breathe as they moved now and again and showed up abeam or off my bow. Two hours tacking against a sea's tide, but much with my own. Then just barely enough air to get back out of the mouth of the Benjamin River, and even more slowly drift East down the Reach, back along the mainland shore to the harbor, the mooring, the yard. A splendor.*

~

Festina.

By the late 1990s, some of the harbingers of the disease that was to take Booth's life began to emerge. The sustained and sustaining forty-year correspondence with Sue Ely, often numbering four or five letters per month, tailed off dramatically. Booth was more likely to send articles of interest or reviews of his poetry or announcements of awards than he was to write the long and self-revealing letters they had exchanged in the past. Peter Davis, who was in the process of renovating the harborfront home in Castine he had purchased, noticed that Booth had become "particularly distant"; when he asked Philip for recommendations for local carpenters, plumbers, and painters, Margaret was really the one who responded in helpful ways. Linda Fidnick remembers the struggles that her father-in-law experienced in telling stories at the dinner table, ones that in years past had been part of a delightful repertoire that he conveyed with humor and polish: "He was a wonderful storyteller; he knew how to shape and pace each story in order to hold your attention. He always knew when to finish. But those kinds of awarenesses were beginning to fail—and his stories would go on and on, seemingly without a resolution or a point. Someone else would have to gently intervene and point this out to him, or, more often, finish the story for him."[16]

A diagnosis of Alzheimer's disease, very difficult news for anyone to absorb, must have been an especially cruel irony for "the word man." Margaret's most vivid memories of her husband are of him sitting, often for hours, alone at his desk, "striving for the right words." "He was driven," she says quietly, "as all serious artists are, to *get it right*." When the diagnosis came, he called a number of his closest friends and fellow poets (including Maxine Kumin and Richard Wilbur) to convey the news personally. As Wilbur remembers, "He called me to say good-bye when the doctor told him he had Alzheimer's; I rose as best I could to so sad and sudden an occasion, and hope to have made my long affection plain."[17]

In that haunting way art sometimes anticipates life, Booth wrote the poem "Heading Out" almost a decade before his diagnosis.

Heading Out

Beyond here there's no map.
How you get there is where
you'll arrive; how, dawn by
dawn, you can see your way
clear: in ponds, sky, just as
woods you walk through give
to fields. And rivers: beyond
all burning, you'll cross on bridges
you've long lugged with you.
Whatever your route, go lightly,
toward light. Once you give away
all save necessity, all's
mostly well: what you used to
believe you owned is nothing,
nothing beside how you've come
to feel. You've no need now
to give in or give out: the way
you're going your body seems
willing. Slowly as it may
otherwise tell you, whatever
it comes to you're bound to know.

Poet Cleopatra Mathis, who came to Dartmouth College in 1982 to found the creative writing program, came to know Booth in his later years. Her interactions with him illumine a chapter in his life that other sources, except the poems themselves, fail to record.

> *My first introduction to Philip Booth came when I received a postcard from Castine shortly after the publication of my first book.* Aerial View of Louisiana *was published in 1979 and Philip wrote a very sweet and encouraging note, congratulating me on writing a good book. I was young, shy, probably awkward at that time and was surprised that he had taken the time to seek me out. I don't think I even responded.*
>
> *But in 1983, after the publication of my second book, another card arrived. By then I was at Dartmouth and Philip mentioned casually that he had "some connections" there, but I had no idea that he was a Dartmouth graduate, or that his father had taught in the English Department.*
>
> *I taught my poetry workshops in the Poetry Room in Sanborn House, and one day one of my students came into class to report that there was "an older gentleman" sitting on one of the couches outside. I went out to investigate and it was Philip—who then came in, introduced himself, said hello to the students, and made some kind and generous remarks about all of us pulling together, studying and writing poetry, in this common enterprise. Thereafter, whenever he and Margaret were back for a visit to Hanover, he would stop in, usually visiting the class.*
>
> *I saw him the most frequently when he and Margaret moved back to Hanover. Although he had lost the ability to bring up certain words, he was not aphasic. Sometimes Margaret would drop him off and he could move independently through Dartmouth's familiar corridors, sometimes turning up at my two o'clock poetry workshop. One day when he arrived I said, "Don't you want to come in and say hello to the students?" He was eager to do that and I expected to say, "This is Philip Booth, he's a fine poet and is visiting today." And that would be that.*

But Philip moved to the front of the room and began to talk about poetry, its difficulties and challenges. If he couldn't bring up a word he'd pantomime it. For example, he said: "Poetry is exacting, very hard to ______ [and pantomimed the act of writing]." Every few sentences or so he would look out to the students and ask, "Questions?" Everybody listened intently. When he finished, he gave a little bow and went around to shake each student's hand.

Whether his illness created the conditions for greater empathy, more layered connections with others, or whether those capacities developed much earlier, I do believe that his later poems reflect a deepening sense of our connections with others. They are more emotionally complex, more complicated metaphorically. He may be writing from the same location, Castine, but the "he" who is seeing Castine is writing from a deeper perspective.

His early work, notable for its short, compressed lines, was not, I think, something he deliberately chose in order to conceal things, but rather was an embodiment of his natural "voice." We all have our own natural rhythms, our own "breath units." My breath unit is four or five beats to the line. Philip's was three or four beats to the line. It was his, his voice, and he had to claim it. What grew more complex was the treatment of and perspective on his subjects.

Philip also had a trait I really admired: he honored generations of poets who had gone before. He saw us all involved in a "common enterprise," each generation standing on the shoulders of the previous generation. My generation of poets revered the poets of Philip's generation: they were "our parents." I find that the generation behind me doesn't wish to be "beholden" to anybody, "derivative" of anybody, and so they are much more dismissive. That, to my mind, is a huge loss.[18]

Several triumphs remained: On November 23, 1996, Dartmouth College honored the ninetieth year of Richard Eberhart, Dartmouth alumnus and professor for more than four decades, and Booth's good friend and

Poets gather to celebrate Richard Eberhart's 90th birthday at Dartmouth College, 1996: Allen Ginsberg, Maxine Kumin, Galway Kinnell, Richard Eberhart, Daniel Hoffman, Donald Hall, Philip Booth.

frequent summer visitor. A striking image of that gathering remains, underscoring a community of poets with bonds deeper than simply the intersections of time and place: Eberhart standing in the center and flanked on the left by Allen Ginsberg, Maxine Kumin, and Galway Kinnell—and flanked on the right by Daniel Hoffman, Donald Hall, and Philip Booth. In 1999, Booth published in a single volume a collected and new set of poems, titled *Lifelines: Selected Poems 1950–1999*. It won the 2001 Poets' Prize, awarded annually for the best book of poetry by a living American poet two years prior to the award year. Since the prize is donated by a committee of twenty American poets who also serve as judges, the honor must have felt especially affirming. Additionally, the "new poems," ones presumably written even within the shadow of Alzheimer's, are among his most seamlessly executed and most life-affirming.

Again, the Solstice

Still.
A stillness.
Not a storm's eye

or its afterlife.
Not the closed quiet
of fog. Only this

high June sky, far
inland, its five
clouds stilled,

the long light
evening. Rooted,
some hundred feet

from the back lot's
hundred-foot pine,
the two of us,

immersed in time
with the tree,
open ourselves to

be touched by light,
light becoming
and gone, gone

and becoming. Moved,
under the tree's
tall stillness,

we let our lives,
lived at groundlevel,
heighten; as the

planet starts to
tilt back toward
dark, we see

how light informs
the tree: at the
utmost tip of its

every branch, the tips,
only now, are just
beginning to candle.

If Philip Booth's poetic development was prompted by the effort "not to tell lies," how might one describe his discoveries, his "truths"? An essential connection to the earth, to nature—including human nature—was one. He wanted to create poems that could look "both up and down" as well as "in and out," poems rooted in the natural landscape that also explored the inner terrain of life as he lived it. Surely it is no accident that the subtitle to his book of prose reflections is *Outlooks and Insights on How Poems Happen*. Nor is his remark in a Wellesley classroom that Oedipus "lost his outlook, but gained insight," which fifty-eight years later still burns in the memory of Peter Davis.

Using his old mentor's coordinates, Booth wrote: "'In deep' and 'out far' are, in Frost's work, the prime foci of his search for any outlook that might provide insight." The narrator in Frost's "Stopping by Woods on a Snowy Evening" chooses to keep familiar "promises" rather than succumbing to the woods that are temptingly "lovely" but also "dark and deep." But, Booth added admiringly, "In a longer poem, 'The Star-Splitter,' [the narrator] repeatedly looks through the telescope of a friend . . . in order, like Frost, to look out far, 'To satisfy a lifelong curiosity / About our place among the infinities.'"[19]

How do we discover our place among the infinities? For Booth that discovery comes from understanding our "relations"—to one another, to nature, to our own essential selves: "It has something to do with my own inmost being, not my heart, not my mind, but my total self; it has something to do with how a human being measures against all that surrounds him. Against all that is within himself, against all that exists in relation to him."[20] Perhaps he catches this feeling most memorably in the closing lines (and spatial relationships of those lines) of the poem "Relations":

by how
    to each other
we're held, we keep

from spinning out
    by how to each other
we hold.

Patrick Walker would add compassion, in all its complexity, to the process of discovering "our place among the infinities": "Philip wanted poems that made life more bearable, that connect us with the life-affirming essences, whether they be found in nature or human nature. To me, a key phrase in Philip's journey appears in a poem called "Chances" when he writes:

love's
transformative; while waves
reshape the beaches where they end,
love remains the mystery
love, in us, informs.

I think that's what he discovered, that "love, in us, informs."[21]

~

The late poems, especially, reveal that loyalty to place derives not simply from history, birthright, and circumstance but from "our need to be at home on earth." As Margaret Booth puts it, "Castine was the only home that I think Philip ever felt was his natural place. He always wanted to be there. He loved the straightforwardness of the people and their affection toward him." Peter Davis adds, "Place and home for Philip Booth equaled Castine. Anyplace else felt like a Letter from a Distant Land; he felt exiled when not in Castine." As Stephen Dunn remembers, "What Philip Booth communicated to those of us learning to find our way as poets was that writing poetry is an extension of one's life, a way of exploring what it felt like to be alive in one's body in a certain place at a certain time."

In lines like these from a late poem titled "Coming To," Booth reclaimed the names of local wildflowers and trees, a legacy of a Castine childhood—made more memorable by his mother's careful naming. Her lessons in recognizing and naming what was wild and beautiful in Castine prefigured his own.

Coming To

Coming to woods in light spring rain,
I know I am not too late.

In my week
of walking down from White Mountains,
I dreamt I might die before
familiar woods woke me.

Come slowly,
the way leaves come, I've arrived at
their turnings: from bronze, gold, wine
to all greens, as they let sun in
to tug them toward light.

Come again now
to woods as they've grown, hardwood
and soft, birch, hemlock, and oak
I walk into my boyhood,
back to
my mother,
the mother who took me in hand

to steer me across back fields to the woods.
Over and over, she slowed to give me
the local names: swampmaple, shadblow,
hackmatack, pine.

Given those woods,
trees renewed in me now, I've begun
to know I'm older than all
but the tallest stands.

Under trees,
I discover my mother's old namings
beginning to bloom: bloodroot,
hepatica, bunchberry, trillium;

in air
so quiet the flowers barely move,
I shiver a little, over and over.
I listen to trout lily, violet, jack-
in-the-pulpit, spring beauty.

I let my head bow as I name them.

What Booth honors in his life's journey, what he "bows" to, is often caught in images from the natural world: the names of native wildflowers taught to him by his mother when he was a boy, the sharing of "an odd salad" with the two does who visit the backyard in Castine, the Arctic tern he encounters on a sailing trip, shortly after reading naturalist Barry Lopez's *Arctic Dreams.* As he records:

> *When I first read the preface to Arctic Dreams and found Barry Lopez recalling a summer evening when he came down from a Brooks Range ridge to walk among the nesting birds on the tundra, and found himself bowing to their fecund presence, their vulnerability, their courage, I knew I was in the presence of a man who was reporting back to my local dailiness a dream of where I had never been. Yet within my own psychic and geographic range*

I, too, have for years nodded my admiration to birds defending their territory. And on local shores, near the Equinox, when plovers and peeps in mid-migration are feeding at the ebb-tide's edge, I have seen what Lopez stunningly knows as a North light that "comes down over the land, like breath, like breathing."

Sailing a small boat out into the bay in that same season, I now and then touch the long bill of my cap to salute an Arctic tern, knowing that his sleek head contains a navigation system which will take him across the Atlantic, and down the African coast, and out into the Antarctic Ocean before he flies back (a round trip of some twenty thousand miles) to fish these waters again.

All such engaging moments are a primal joy; I'm being my solo self in sudden company with creatures who inhabit air or water in a way I cannot, creatures in whose presence I feel rather than think, being charged by the presence of their otherness to be in myself more alive."[22]

At the same time, Booth bows to the human community of which he is a part and which has integral connections to the natural world. For what he honors in the naming of the wildflowers is not simply the access to the natural world they provide, but the access to his mother's nurturing care in his childhood. He bows to the undergraduate creative writing students in Cleopatra Mathis's poetry workshop as they set out on their own navigational journeys, difficult and rewarding as they will be. He honors, in "Presence," "our skin no more or less than that of redwing, / rainbow, star-nose, or whitethroat, enfolded like us / in the valleys and waves of this irrefutable planet."

While Booth was quick to reject unearned affirmations, his poems, particularly in the last decades of his writing life, pulse with a quiet but insistent lyricism, suggesting that we are capable of imagining our affinities with one another and discovering our home on this earth. Philip Booth did not simply live in Castine and use it as his muse. He belonged to it. In finding the language to evoke its austerity and amplitude, its stoicism and generosity, he discovered his own centering place from which to look in, his own vantage point from which to look out.

Coda

One day, nearing the end of my research, Margot Booth sent me a photograph "of Dad's truck, heading down Main Street, complete with a newly cut Christmas tree from Cold Knoll." The context she offered for this photo encapsulates, for me, the shape of Booth's life journey. She writes:

> *Dad had an old truck that he would drive up and down Main Street and all over town for many years. On the back he had a bumper sticker, one of those Army stickers that suggested that you should "Be all that you can be. . . . Join the Army." Dad had cut out the part about joining the Army, leaving just the instruction BE ALL THAT YOU CAN BE. He loved that notion, which meant to him, I think, trying to feel and learn and know yourself and relate to others as much as you can. He was keenly aware of the "as much as you can" part. He actually had done a good deal of*

> *thinking about every word on that bumper sticker, as poets will. Once he told me to note that the author of that little phrase did not say "Be all that you are meant to be," or "Be all that you are," or "Be all that you want to be," but wrote, "Be all that you can be," implying, Dad thought, that people have limitations, so we all have to do the best we can to be all that we can, given our limitations. I think this represents a big part of the essence of him: the dynamic tension between his anxieties and limitations, and his acute awareness of them and his big, grand spirit."*[1]

In his efforts to "be all that he could be," Booth did not, either by deliberate choice or inclination, join any of the "schools" of poets writing in the 1960s, '70s, and '80s: the postmodernists, the confessional school, the beats, the surrealists. Instead, his unique strengths lay in his powers of observation and interpretation. In the act of noticing crucial details and arranging them on the page, he came to grasp—and sculpt—their meaning. He wrote poems "to discover what they will become."[2]

But if Booth was not by temperament "a joiner," he was an attentive, engaged man of his times. And what electric times they were. A member of what Tom Brokaw called the Greatest Generation, he returned from military service to a country about to experience a rapid-fire succession of soul-searching convulsions: the Cold War, Korea, the civil rights movement, Vietnam, the Balkans. As a young poet he had the great good fortune to live close to Boston among a brilliant circle of poets, many of whom were also embarking on notable careers. He lived and wrote at a time when statesmen and philosophers sought the advice of poets: an invitation to dinner from Mary McCarthy next door in Castine could result in sitting next to Hannah Arendt, visiting for the weekend; a particularly promising sailing day could yield an unexpected visit from Ted Kennedy, up from Hyannis, talking foreign policy with Robert Lowell over drinks in Booth's Shed. Mindful of the generous mentoring he had received from Robert Frost, he, in turn, taught and mentored some of the most promising poets of the next generation, among them a Pulitzer Prize winner. If he was the beneficiary of many fomenting collisions—artistic, historic, educational—he was also the agent of his own development. In exploring the heart of Castine, he learned the difference between residing in a place and abiding in it, a gift his poems offer to any attentive reader.

For after all, poems are acts of connection—seeking communion with a reader who can take the poem in, and be calmed, or challenged to action, or transported by it.

Philip Booth's poems are as complicated, as resonant, and as enduring as our capacity to receive them. Take in the last poem in Philip Booth's final volume —set at sea, returning to the home harbor, attended by love—and abide in it.

Passage without Rites

Homing, inshore, from far off-soundings.
Night coming on. Sails barely full.

The wind,
in its dying, too light to lift us against
the long ebb.

My two fingers, light
on the tiller, try to believe I feel
the turned tide.

Hard to tell. Maybe,
as new currents pressure the rudder,
I come to sense

the keel beginning
to shape the flow of the sea. Deep
and aloft, it's close

to dark.
No stars yet. Only the risen nightwind,
as we tack into its warmth,

tells us
we'll make our homeport. Strange,
angling into the dark,

                    to think
how a mainsail's camber reflects
the arc of the keel,

                    their dynamics
reversing whenever we tack.
You call from below,

                    hand up coffee,
check the glow of the compass, and
raise an eye to Arcturus,

                    just now
beginning to shine. All over again,
all over, our old bodies

                    breathe
the old mysteries: the long night
still to go, small bow-waves

                    playing
a little *nachtmusik*; stars beyond stars
flooding our inmost eyes.

                    And voices,
now, come out of the dark,
deeply sounding our own.

Endnotes

Introduction

1 Philip Booth, "Frost's Empty Spaces," as collected in *Trying to Say It: Outlooks and Insights on How Poems Happen* (Ann Arbor: The University of Michigan Press, 1996), p. 59.
2 Booth, interview for *The Castine Patriot*, 1980, as quoted in "Philip Booth, remembered by Dixie Gray," *The Castine Historical Society Newsletter*, Spring 2008.
3 Booth, *Trying to Say It*, p. 35.
4 Henry L. Miller, letter to the author, April 30, 2014.
5 Wesley McNair, "Boothed," a chapter in *Mapping the Heart: Reflections on Place and Poetry* (Pittsburgh: Carnegie Mellon University Press, 2003), p. 99.
6 Booth, *Trying to Say It*, p. 98.

First Lesson

1 Philip Conkling, "Local Knowledge in Hard Country," interview with Philip Booth, *Island Journal*, 1988, p. 43.
2 Ibid.
3 Interview with Margaret Booth, January 21, 2014.
4 Philip Booth, *Trying to Say It*, pp. 116–117.
5 Letter to the author from Margot Booth, September 4, 2014.
6 Peter Davison, *The Fading Smile: Poets in Boston from Robert Lowell to Sylvia Plath* (New York: W. W. Norton & Company, 1994), p. 21.
7 Letter to the author from Donald Hall, August 28, 2013.
8 Davison, *The Fading Smile,* p. 125.
9 Ibid.
10 Conkling, *Island Journal,* p. 43.
11 Ibid., p. 44.
12 Booth, *Trying to Say It,* p. 56.
13 Interview with Patrick Walker, August 8, 2014.
14 Davison, *The Fading Smile*, p. 128.
15 Philip Booth, "Relations," an interview by Stephen Dunn, 1985, as collected in *Trying to Say It*, p. 126.
16 Conkling, *Island Journal*, p. 43.
17 Interview with Stephen Dunn, *Trying to Say It*, p. 127.
18 Ibid., p. 126.
19 Interview with Carol Booth, January 21, 2014.
20 Rachel Berghash, "Chances of Survival: Philip Booth in Conversation," 1988, as collected in *Trying to Say It,* p. 115.

21 Interview with Peter Davis, September 22, 2013.
22 Letter to the author from Stephen Dunn, September 16, 2013.
23 Letter to the author from Maxine Kumin, September 3, 2013.
24 Letter to the author from Richard Wilbur, August 28, 2013.

Not to Tell Lies

1 Philip Booth, "Summers in Castine/Contact Prints: 1955–1965, collected in *Trying to Say It*, pp. 20–21. Lowell biographer Ian Hamilton explains the origins of Lowell's nickname, "Cal," in this way: "Fighting back was one of the few things Robert Lowell got high marks for during his school days. He is remembered as dark, menacing, belligerent; always bigger, stronger, shaggier than his contemporaries." (*Robert Lowell: A Biography*, p. 14.) Given this description, it is hardly surprising that his schoolmates called him "Caliban" (the half-human, half-beast in Shakespeare's *The Tempest*), or later "Caligula" (the tyrannical Roman emperor). The nickname "Cal" stuck with him throughout his life.
2 Peter Davison describes the nature of the early relationship between Booth and Lowell in *The Fading Smile*, p. 127.
3 Ibid.
4 Booth, *Trying to Say It*, p. 24.
5 Interview with Margaret Booth, January 21, 2014.
6 Booth, *Trying to Say It*, pp. 35–37.
7 Stephen Dunn, "Philip Booth (1925–2007): A Remembrance," *Stone Canoe* (2008).
8 Dunn, "Larry Levis in Syracuse," *Blackbird: An Online Journal of Literature and the Arts*, Fall 2006.
9 Booth, "Compass," supplement to *The Castine Patriot* (March 21, 1991), p. 1.
10 Interview with Robin Booth, September 20, 2014.
11 Stephen Dunn, *Walking Light: Memoirs and Essays on Poetry* (Rochester: Boa Editions, Ltd., 2001), pp. 142–143.
12 Interview with Patrick Walker, August 8, 2014.
13 Booth, *Trying to Say It*, p. 136.
14 Ibid., p. 73.
15 Interview with Carol Booth, January 21, 2014.
16 Booth, *Trying to Say It*, p. 74.
17 Ibid., p. 108.
18 Letter to the author from Carol Booth, September 27, 2013.
19 Interview with Peter Davis, September 23, 2013.
20 Interview with Carol Allen, May 10, 2014.
21 Henry L. Miller, "Remembering a Maine Poet," *The Bangor News*, July 12, 2007.

22 Booth, *Trying to Say It*, pp. 26–27.
23 Ibid., p. 34.
24 Ibid., pp. 38–39.

Heading Out

1 Interview with Robin Booth, September 20, 2014.
2 Caroline Pinkston, Chapel Talk (excerpts), St. Andrews Episcopal School (Austin, Texas), March 19, 2013.
3 Interview with Philip Conkling, February 10, 2015.
4 Interview with Ben Bradley, February 10, 2015.
5 Philip Booth, "Leaning All the Way Out," *Christian Science Monitor*, February 20, 1987.
6 Philip Conkling, *Island Journal*, p. 43.
7 Booth, "Selected Fragments," from *Ploughshares*, 17, no. 1 (May 1991).
8 Stephen Dunn, interview with Philip Booth, *Trying to Say It*, p. 145.
9 Ibid., p. 132.
10 Booth, "A Distinctive Voice," *Trying to Say It*, p. 69.
11 Wesley McNair, *Mapping the Heart: Reflections on Place and Poetry* (Pittsburgh: Carnegie Mellon University Press, 2003), p. 96.
12 Ibid., p. 101.
13 Rollie McKenna was a fine arts photographer known for her beautifully crafted portraits of poets and novelists. Her reputation soared after she published a series of memorable photographs of poet Dylan Thomas, wearing his characteristic rumpled turtleneck, peering out from under a pile of unruly curls. She drove from her home in Connecticut to Castine on a number of summer occasions, shooting images of Lowell, McCarthy, and Booth and, in the process, became Booth's good friend.
14 Booth, *Trying to Say It*, p. 69.
15 Interview with David Hatch, March 8, 2015.
16 Interview with Linda Fidnick, July 16, 2014.
17 Letter to the author from Richard Wilbur, August 28, 2013.
18 Interview with Cleopatra Mathis, August 27, 2014.
19 Booth, *Trying to Say It*, p. 13.
20 Ibid., p. 137.
21 Interview with Patrick Walker, August 8, 2014.
22 Booth, *Trying to Say It*, pp. 5–6.

Coda

1 Letter from Margot Booth, September 14, 2014.
2 Jim Laughton, quoting Booth in "From Ache in the Arch to the Edge," *Syracuse Post-Standard*, April 12, 1983.

Selected Readings

The following books may be of interest to readers who wish to explore further the work of Philip Booth and his contemporaries, as well as the intersections between writing and a sense of place.

Berry, Wendell. *The Long-Legged House.* New York: Harcourt, Brace & World, 1969.

__. *The Gift of Good Land: Further Essays Cultural and Agricultural.* San Francisco: North Point Press, 1981.

Booth, Philip. *Trying to Say It: Outlooks and Insights on How Poems Happen.* Ann Arbor: University of Michigan Press, 1996.

__. *Lifelines: Selected Poems 1950–1999.* New York: Viking, 1999.

Brightman, Carol. *Writing Dangerously: Mary McCarthy and Her World.* New York: Clarkson Potter, 1992.

Cunningham, Michael. *Land's End: A Walk in Provincetown.* New York: Crown, 2002.

Davison, Peter. *The Fading Smile: Poets in Boston from Robert Lowell to Sylvia Plath.* New York: W. W. Norton, 1994.

Dillard, Annie. *Pilgrim at Tinker Creek.* New York: Harper's Magazine Press (reprint), 1974.

__. *An American Childhood.* New York: Harper and Row, 1987.

Dunn, Stephen. *Walking Light: Memoirs and Essays on Poetry.* Rochester, New York: Boa Editions, 2001.

Finch, Robert. *Common Ground: A Naturalist's Cape Cod.* New York: W. W. Norton, 1994.

Haines, John. *Living Off the Country.* Ann Arbor: University of Michigan Press, 1982.

Hall, Donald. *String Too Short to Be Saved: Recollections of Summers on a New England Farm.* Boston: David R. Godine, 1960, Reprint: 1981.

__. *Seasons at Eagle Pond.* Boston: Houghton Mifflin, 1987.

Hampl, Patricia. *A Romantic Education.* Boston: Houghton Mifflin, 1981.

Hamilton, Ian. *Robert Lowell: A Biography.* New York: Random House, 1982.

Hardwick, Elizabeth. *Herman Melville.* New York: Viking, 2000.

Kiernan, Frances. *Seeing Mary Plain: A Life of Mary McCarthy.* New York: W. W. Norton, 2000.

Klinkenborg, Verlyn. *The Rural Life.* Boston: Little, Brown, 2003.

Kumin, Maxine. *In Deep: Country Essays.* New York: Viking, 1987.

__. *Always Beginning: Essays on a Life in Poetry.* Port Townsend, Washington: Copper Canyon Press, 2000.

Kunitz, Stanley. *A Kind of Order, a Kind of Folly: Essays and Conversations.* Boston: Atlantic Monthly Press, Little, Brown, 1975.

__ (with Genine Lentine). *The Wild Braid: A Poet Reflects on a Century in the Garden*. New York: W. W. Norton, 2005.

Lopez, Barry. *Arctic Dreams, Imagination and Desire in a Northern Landscape.* New York: Charles Scribner's Sons, 1986.

Mariani, Paul. *Lost Puritan: A Life of Robert Lowell.* New York: W. W. Norton, 1996.

McCarthy, Mary. *Memories of a Catholic Girlhood.* New York: Harcourt Brace and Company, 1957.

Norris, Kathleen. *Dakota: A Spiritual Geography.* New York: Ticknor & Fields, 1993.

Oliver, Mary. *Long Life: Essays and Other Writings.* Boston: Da Capo Press, 2005.

Sanders, Scott Russell. *Staying Put: Making a Home in a Restless World.* Boston: Beacon Press, 1993.

Sarton, May. *Journal of a Solitude.* New York: W. W. Norton, 1973.

__. *The House by the Sea.* New York: W. W. Norton, 1977.

Williams, Terry Tempest. *An Unspoken Hunger: Stories from the Field.* New York: Pantheon, 1994.

__. *Refuge: An Unnatural History of Family and Place.* New York: Vintage, 2001.

Archival Collections

The papers of Philip Booth can be accessed through the Rauner Special Collections at Dartmouth College. The collection includes correspondence with family, poets, and writers, including Ted Hughes, Sylvia Plath, W. D. Snodgrass, David Bradley, Robert Lowell, May Sarton, E. B. White, William Carlos Williams, Galway Kinnell, W. S. Merwin, Gary Snyder, Anne Sexton, Maxine Kumin, Stephen Dunn, Richard Eberhart, Adrienne Rich, Robert Bly, Donald Hall, James Merrill, Hayden Carruth, and many others. The collection also includes manuscripts, typescripts, and gallery proofs of poems and prose by Booth, as well as newspaper clippings, photographs, audiocassette tapes with readings and interviews, and books with annotations by Booth.

A number of photographs, interviews, and articles about the Booth family history in Castine; the years when the lives of Booth, Lowell, Hardwick, and McCarthy intersected in Castine; and Booth's avid interest in sailing and boatbuilding can be accessed through the Castine Historical Society. A rich oral history of Castine, composed of interviews with longtime Castine residents, spans a forty-year period. Most recently, Dr. Ken Scheer has extended that history by recording and editing a video "living history" of Castine, now available through the Castine Historical Society website.

Permissions

"First Lesson," "Chart 1203," "Storm in a Formal Garden," "How to See Deer," "Not to Tell Lies," "This Day After Yesterday," "Eaton's Boatyard," "Building Her," "Before Sleep," "Heading Out," "Presence," "Coming To," "Again, the Solstice," "Passage Without Rites," from *Lifelines: Selected Poems 1950–1999*, by Philip Booth, copyright © 1999 by Philip Booth. Used by permission of Viking Books, an imprint of Penguin Publishing Group, a division of Penguin Random House LLC.

Wesley McNair, excerpts from *Mapping the Heart: Reflections on Poetry and Place,* copyright © 2003 by Wesley McNair. Reprinted with the permission of The Permissions Company, Inc., on behalf of Carnegie Mellon University Press.

Excerpts from Richard P. Jackson's interview with Philip Booth, "Lives We Keep Wanting to Know," published in *Poetry Miscellany* no. 8 (1978). Used by permission of Richard P. Jackson.

Excerpts from Stephen Dunn's essay, "Larry Levis in Syracuse," originally published in *Blackbird: An Online Journal of Literature and the Arts,*" fall 2006. Used by permission of Stephen Dunn.

Excerpts from Rachel Berghash's "Chances of Survival," an interview with Philip Booth that originally appeared in *The American Poetry Review* in 1989. Used by permission of Rachel Berghash.

Stephen Dunn, excerpts from *Walking Light: Memoirs and Essays on Poetry,* copyright © 2001 by Stephen Dunn. Reprinted with the permission of The Permissions Company, Inc., on behalf of BOA Editions, Ltd., www.boaeditions.org.

Excerpts from Stephen Dunn's interview with Philip Booth, "Relations," originally published in *New England Review,* winter 1986. Used by permission of Stephen Dunn.

Excerpts from Stephen Dunn's "A Remembrance," originally published in *Stone Canoe,* 2008. Used by permission of Stephen Dunn.

Excerpts from Philip Booth's essay, "Distances/Shallows/Deeps: Field Notes from an East-Facing Window at the Cold End of a Long Maine Winter," originally published in *The Ohio Review, Art and Nature Issue* (winter 1993). Used by permission of the *New Ohio Review.*

Excerpts from Philip Booth's essay "Robert Lowell's Summers in Castine," originally published in *Salmagundi* in spring of 1977. Used by permission of *Salmagundi* magazine.

Excerpts from Philip Booth's "Selected Fragments, 1987," originally published in *Ploughshares* 17 (May 1991). Used by permission of Margaret Booth.

The poem "Wanting" by Philip Booth, originally published in *Ploughshares*

(1988) and later reprinted in the *Island Journal.* Used by permission of Margaret Booth.

Excerpts from "Writing with Light," Philip Booth's essay on the work of Maine photographer Jeff Dworsky, published in the *Island Journal* (1992). Used by permission of Peter Ralston.

Excerpts from "Local Knowledge in Hard Country," an interview with Philip Booth by Philip Conkling, published in *Island Journal* (1988). Used by permission of Philip Conkling.

Excerpts from "Leaning All the Way Out," an essay by Philip Booth, originally published in *Christian Science Monitor* (February 20, 1987). Used by permission of Robin Booth.

Excerpts from *The Fading Smile: Poets in Boston from Robert Lowell to Sylvia Plath,* by Peter Davison, copyright © 1994 by Peter Davison. Used by permission of Alfred A. Knopf, an imprint of Knopf Doubleday Publishing Group, a division of Penguin Random House LLC.

Photo Credits

Thanks to the Rauner Special Collections Library, Dartmouth College Library, for permission to use the following photos and letters: young Philip Booth with Robert Frost, young Robert Lowell, letters from Ted Kennedy to Philip Booth, letter from Maxine Kumin to Philip Booth, Philip Booth's telegram to Elizabeth Hardwick on the death of Robert Lowell, letter from Philip Booth to Robert Lowell.

Thanks to the Castine Historical Society for permission to use the photo of the poets gathered to celebrate Richard Eberhart's 90th birthday, the photo of Mary McCarthy, and the photo of Robert Lowell and Elizabeth Hardwick.

Thanks to Peter Davis for permission to use photos of his wife and family from his private collection.

Special thanks to Peter Ralston for permission to use "The Poet," his photo of Philip Booth that graces the cover; it was taken in Castine in 1987.

Thanks to Pamela Peterson for providing photos of the exterior and interior of Eaton's Boatyard as well as Philip Booth's gravestone.

Thanks to Sarah Bauhan for providing the photos of Main Street's plunge to the harbor, Philip Booth's studio, and the exterior of the Booth home.

Special thanks to Robert Floyd for the author's photo.

All other photos are used by permission of Margaret Booth and the Booth family, generously shared from their own private collections.

Acknowledgments

In the absence of a full-fledged critical study of Philip Booth's work or a definitive biography of his life, this portrait emerged from three primary sources: a careful rereading of Booth's poems and prose pieces; first-person accounts drawn from family, friends, former students, and fellow poets; and archival materials housed at Dartmouth College's Rauner Special Collections Library in Hanover, New Hampshire, and at the Castine Historical Society in Maine. Philip Booth's habit of keeping meticulous records, described in working notebooks, drafts of poems, precisely annotated photograph albums, and a voluminous correspondence, added depth and dimensionality to gathering "the facts." I made three trips to Hanover and three extended trips to Castine, prompted partly by research, but also by the desire to walk, watch, listen, and absorb the "gift of place."

I'm grateful for the help of Barbara Krieger at Dartmouth's Rauner Special Collections Library and Paige Lilly at the Castine Historical Society, who guided my research efforts in their collections. Carol Allen, Ben Bradley, Philip Conkling, Peter Davis, Stephen Dunn, Kathy Eaton, Donald Hall, David Hatch, Maxine Kumin, Cleopatra Mathis, Wesley McNair, Henry L. Miller, Peter Ralston, and Richard Wilbur took the time to contribute vivid memories of Philip Booth in his various roles as teacher, poet, bon vivant, sailor, and meditative man. Sue Ely, a student of Booth's at Wellesley, who thereafter carried on a remarkable correspondence and friendship with him stretching over forty years, generously shared many letters.

Family members Patrick Walker, Caroline Pinkston, Linda Fidnick, Margot Booth, Carol Booth, and Robin Booth offered their stories and photographs, and, perhaps even more memorably, their honest assessments of a complicated and deeply layered father, father-in-law, and grandfather. Theirs was a difficult assignment, handled with grace.

Undaunted by the task of driving to Castine to scan and then restore some crucial photographs that had suffered fading and damage over time, publisher Sarah Bauhan and art director Henry James designed a book that allows a reader to envision not only the home ground of Philip Booth, but the specifics of place and the spirit of a time when American poetry was vibrantly alive.

Special thanks to Sarah Bauhan, Peter Ralston, and Pamela Peterson for on-site photographs that capture Philip Booth and the places he loved and brought to life in his work.

My own family, in particular Mary Jeanne Mullen, Bob Buck, Tori and Sophia, Tim Mullen, Maggie Mullen, Dan and Andrew, offer bedrock support for my writing endeavors and in my daily life. Pam Peterson and Alice took this journey with me, sometimes metaphorically and sometimes literally; they help me see with fresh eyes—and joy always rides with Alice.

Margaret Booth was not only generous in sharing her time and rich storehouse of memories—she also emerged as a pivotal player in almost every narrative of her husband's life and work that I encountered. When Philip was asked how he had managed to complete his first book of poems while teaching full time and living in a small house with three very young children, he said, after a short pause, "The answer is Margaret, I'm sure." *The answer is Margaret, I'm sure* became a kind of leitmotif, appearing in interview after interview, in story after story, regardless of the narrator. Rarely is the dedication of a book so richly deserved.

FESTINA